How to find what yo
The Little Penguin I

If you want a quick overview of what's in this book, then you can look at the **Brief Contents** to the left.

If you see a chapter that interests you in this Brief Contents, then you can go to the page number listed or turn to the appropriate **Part opening page** for that general topic. On the back of that page is a detailed list of the contents of that part of the book.

If you want to know more about what's in a particular chapter or part, then you can also find a **detailed table of contents** inside the back cover.

If you want to know where to find help for a very specific issue or if you need to look up a particular term, then you can refer to the **Index** on page 266.

If you need help starting your research paper, refer to **"Five Steps for Planning and Conducting Research"** at the beginning of Part 2.

If you need help with the documentation process, refer to **"Five Steps for Documenting Sources"** at the beginning of Part 3.

If you want information about MLA, APA, CMS, or CSE **documentation styles** for research writing, turn to the first page of the appropriate chapter in Part 3. You will find a complete index of sample citations for each documentation style.

You will also find **more help** at the back of this book:

- A list of **Common Errors** of grammar, punctuation, and mechanics that many writers make
- A **Revision Guide** of editing and proofreading symbols
- A **Glossary** with basic grammatical and usage terms, on page 255.

THE

Little Penguin Handbook

Second Edition

LESTER FAIGLEY

University of Texas at Austin

Longman

New York San Francisco Boston
London Toronto Sydney Tokyo Singapore Madrid
Mexico City Munich Paris Cape Town Hong Kong Montreal

Executive Editor: Lynn M. Huddon
Director of Development: Mary Ellen Curley
Senior Marketing Manager: Susan Stoudt
Production Manager: Savoula Amanatidis
Project Coordination, Text Design, and Electronic Page Makeup: Pre-Press PMG
Senior Cover Design Manager: Nancy Danahy
Cover Photos: Clockwise from top right: Purestock/Jupiter Images; Isu/STOCK4B-RF/Getty Images; Stockbyte/Getty Images; Tim Starkey/iStockphoto; I. Rozenbaum & F. Cirou/PhotoAlto/Jupiter Images; Mike Bentley/iStockphoto; Art Vandalay/Digital Vision/Getty; and Anderson Ross/Blend Images/Jupiter Images.
Photo Researcher: Rona Tuccillo
Senior Manufacturing Buyer: Dennis J. Para
Printer and Binder: R. R. Donnelley and Sons Company—Crawfordsville
Cover Printer: Lehigh-Phoenix Color Corp.

For permission to use copyrighted material, grateful acknowledgment is made to the copyright holders on p. 282, which is hereby made part of this copyright page.

Library of Congress Cataloging-in-Publication Data

Faigley, Lester, 1947–
The Little Penguin handbook / Lester Faigley. — [2nd ed.]
p. cm.
Abbreviated version of The Penguin Handbook.
Includes bibliographical references and index.
ISBN 978-0-205-74339-1 (alk. paper)
1. English language—Rhetoric—Handbooks, manuals, etc. 2. English Language—Grammar—Handbooks, manuals, etc. 3. Report writing—Handbooks, manuals, etc. I. Title.
PE1408.F245 2008
808'.042—dc22

2008033715

This book includes 2009 MLA guidelines.

1 2 3 4 5 6 7 8 9 10—DOC—12 11 10 09

Longman
is an imprint of

www.pearsonhighered.com

ISBN-13: 978-0-205-74339-1
ISBN-10: 0-205-74339-0

PART 1

Composing

1 Think as a Writer

Learning to write for specific readers is the key to success in college and beyond.

1a Think About the Process of Communication

Whether you are writing a research paper for a political science course, designing a Web site for a small business, or preparing slides for a sales presentation, you are participating in a complex process. That process—communication—involves the interaction of three essential elements: the writer or speaker, the audience, and the subject. These three elements are often represented by a triangle.

Speaker, subject, and audience are each necessary for an act of communication to occur. These three elements interact with each other. Speakers make adjustments to their presentations of a subject depending on the audience (think of how you talk to small children). Just as speakers adjust to audiences, audiences continually adjust to speakers (think of how your attitude toward speakers changes when they are able to laugh at themselves).

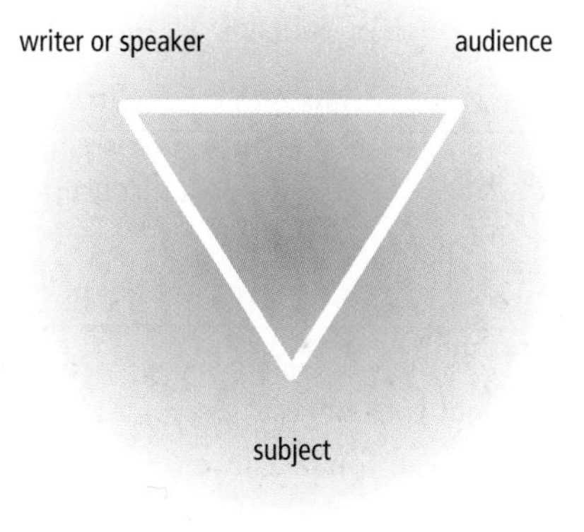

Figure 1.1 The rhetorical triangle

1b Think About Your Audience

In college writing, you often write for readers you know directly, including your classmates and your teachers. In the workplace, you may not always know who is going to read your reports or memos. Ask yourself who will read your writing and think about what kind of information you need to provide to engage them.

UNDERSTAND YOUR AUDIENCE

- Who is most likely to read what you write?
- How much does your audience know about your subject? Are there any key terms or concepts that you will need to explain?
- How interested is your audience likely to be? If they lack interest in your subject, how can you get them engaged?
- What is their attitude likely to be toward your subject? If they hold attitudes different from yours, how can you get them to consider your views?
- What would motivate your audience to want to read what you write?

1c Think About Your Credibility

Some writers begin with credibility because of who they are. Most writers, however, have to convince their readers to keep reading by demonstrating knowledge of their subject and concern with their readers' needs.

BUILD YOUR CREDIBILITY

- How can you convince your audience that you are knowledgeable about your subject? Do you need to do research?
- How can you convince your audience that you have their interests in mind?
- What strategies can you use that will enhance your credibility? Should you cite experts on your subject? Can you acknowledge opposing positions, indicating that you've taken a balanced view on your subject?
- Does the appearance, accuracy, and clarity of your writing give you credibility?

2 Read and View with a Critical Eye

College requires you to think in depth about what you read and see.

2a Become a Critical Reader

You can become a more effective critical reader if you have a set of strategies and use them while you read.

Preview

No subject is ever completely new; it is likely that many people have written and talked about the subject and that many have views on the subject. Begin by asking the following questions:

- Who wrote this material?
- Where did it first appear? In a book, newspaper, magazine, or online?
- What is the topic or issue?
- Where does the writer stand on the topic or issue?
- What else has been written about the topic or issue?
- Why was it written?

Summarize

Make sure you understand exactly what is at issue. Circle any words or references that you don't know and look them up. Summarize by asking yourself these questions:

- What is the writer's main claim or question?
- If I do not find a specific claim, what is the main focus?
- What are the key ideas or concepts that the writer considers?
- What are the key terms? How does the writer define those terms?

Respond

As you read, write down your thoughts. Ask yourself these questions:

- To what points made by the writer should I respond?
- What ideas might be developed or interpreted differently?
- What do I need to look up?

Analyze

On your second reading, analyze the structure using the following questions:

- How is the piece of writing organized?
- What does the writer assume the readers know and believe?
- Where is the evidence? Can you think of contradictory evidence?
- Does the writer acknowledge opposing views? Does the writer deal fairly with opposing views?
- What kinds of sources are cited? Are they thoroughly documented?
- How does the writer represent herself or himself?

2b Become a Critical Viewer

Like critical reading, critical viewing requires you to reflect in depth on what you see. Use the following strategies:

Preview

Critical viewing requires thinking about the context first.

- Who created this image?
- Why was it created?
- Where and when did it first appear?
- What media are used?
- What has been written about the creator or the image?

Respond

Make notes as you view the image with these questions in mind:

- What was my first impression of the image?
- After thinking more—perhaps reading more—about it, how has that first impression changed or expanded?

Analyze

The following analytical questions apply primarily to still images.

- How is the image composed or framed?
- Where do my eyes go first?
- How does the image appeal to the values of the audience?
- Was it intended to serve a purpose besides art or entertainment?

The billboard suggests that this photograph was taken when travel by train was still popular. In fact, it was taken in 1937 by Dorothea Lange (1895–1965), who gave it the title "Toward Los Angeles, California." The lines of the shoulder of the road, the highway, and the telephone poles slope toward a vanishing point on the horizon, giving a sense of great distance. The two figures in dark clothing walking away contrast to a rectangular billboard with a white background and white frame.

Another approach to critical viewing is to analyze the content. In 1937 the United States was in the midst of the Great Depression and a severe drought, which forced many small farmers in middle America to abandon their homes and go to California in search of work. By placing the figures and the billboard beside each other, Lange is able to make an ironic commentary on the lives of well-off and poor Americans during the Depression.

3 Plan Your Writing

Planning begins with thinking about your goals and your readers.

3a Establish Goals and Find a Topic

Often an assignment will contain key words such as *analyze, compare and contrast, define, describe, evaluate,* or *propose* that will guide you.

- **Analyze:** Find connections among a set of facts, events, or readings.
- **Compare and contrast:** Examine how two or more things are alike and how they differ.
- **Define:** Make a claim about how something should be defined.
- **Describe:** Observe carefully and select details.
- **Evaluate:** Argue that something is good, bad, best, or worst, according to criteria that you set out.
- **Propose:** Identify a particular problem and explain why your solution is the best one.

3b Write a Working Thesis

Having a specific focus is the key to writing a strong essay.

Use questions to focus a broad topic

Childhood obesity might be a current and interesting research topic, but it is too broad. Ask questions that will break a big topic into smaller topics.

- Why are children today more obese than children of past generations?
- How has the American food industry contributed to obesity?
- What changes in American culture have contributed to obesity?
- What strategies are effective for preventing childhood obesity?

Consider other angles to expand a narrow topic

Sometimes a topic can become too narrow or limiting. Although candy consumption may be one contributing factor leading to obesity in children, this narrow focus overlooks other factors that together lead to childhood obesity.

- Why do some children eat large amounts of candy yet maintain a healthy weight?
- Children have always eaten candy. Why are children today more obese than children of past generations?
- Even when parents keep kids away from candy, some still gain weight. Why?

Turn your topic into a thesis statement

Your thesis states your main idea. Much of the writing that you will do in college and in your career will have an explicit thesis, usually stated near the beginning. Your thesis should be closely tied to your purpose—to reflect on your own experience, to explain some aspect of your topic, or to argue for a position or course of action.

A reflective thesis

Watching my younger sister's struggles with her weight has taught me that childhood obesity has long-lasting psychological effects.

An informative thesis

Childhood obesity has continued to increase over the past decade despite increasing awareness of its detrimental effects.

A persuasive thesis

Parents must encourage healthy eating and exercise habits in order to reverse the growing trend toward obesity in children.

4 Write a Draft

Skilled writers have strategies for all phases of the writing process.

4a Determine Your Organization

Working outlines

A working outline is more like an initial sketch of how you will arrange the major sections of your essay or report. Jotting down main points and a few subpoints before you begin can be a great help while you are writing.

Formal outlines

A formal outline typically begins with the thesis statement, which anchors the entire outline. Each numbered or lettered item clearly supports the thesis, and the relationship among the items is clear from the outline hierarchy. Roman numerals indicate the highest level; next come capital letters, then Arabic numbers, and finally lowercase letters. The rule to remember when deciding whether you need to use the next level down is that each level must have at least two items: a "1." needs a "2."; an "a." needs a "b." Formal outlines can be helpful because they force you to look carefully at your organization.

Discipline-specific organization

In the social sciences, research reports typically follow a specific organization, with an abstract that gives a brief summary of the contents followed by four main sections and a list of references. This organization allows other researchers to identify information quickly.

1. The **introduction** (identifies the problem, reviews previous research, and states the hypothesis that was tested)
2. The **methods section** (describes how the participants were selected and how the experiment was conducted)

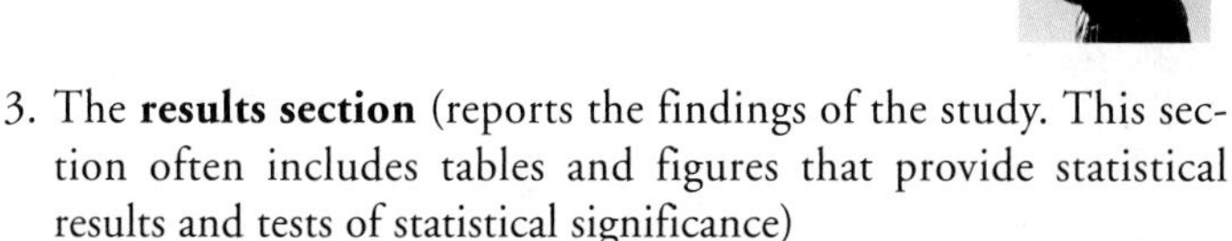

3. The **results section** (reports the findings of the study. This section often includes tables and figures that provide statistical results and tests of statistical significance)
4. The **discussion section** (interprets the findings and often refers to previous research)

For more information on how writing is organized in various disciplines, see Chapter 7.

 Compose a Draft

Essays typically contain an introduction, body, and conclusion. You do not have to draft these parts in that order, though. You may want to begin with your best example, which might be in the third paragraph according to your working outline. The most important thing about drafting is that you feel comfortable and treat yourself kindly. If your inner critic shows up—that little voice in your mind that has nothing encouraging to say—banish it, refute it, write through it.

OVERCOMING WRITER'S BLOCK

- If you have an outline, put it on the computer screen or place it beside you.
- Begin writing what you know best.
- Resist the urge to revise too soon.
- If you get stuck, try working on another section.
- If you are still stuck, talk to someone about what you are trying to write.

5 Compose Paragraphs

Your paragraphs should set out a line of thought for your readers.

Focus Your Paragraphs

Often writers will begin a paragraph with one idea, then other ideas will occur to them while they are writing. Paragraphs confuse readers when they go in different directions. When you revise your paragraphs, check for focus.

Topic sentences

Topic sentences alert readers to the focus of a paragraph and help writers stay on topic. Topic sentences should explain the focus of the paragraph and situate it in the larger argument. Topic sentences, however, do not have to begin paragraphs, and they need not be just one sentence.

5b Write Effective Beginning and Ending Paragraphs

Effective beginning paragraphs convince the reader to read on. They capture the reader's interest and set the tone for the piece.

Start beginning paragraphs with a bang

Try beginning with one of the following strategies to get your reader's attention.

A concisely stated thesis

If the governments of China and Russia don't soon act decisively, snow leopards will be extinct in a few years.

Images

Tons of animal pelts and bones sit in storage at Royal Chitwan National Park in Nepal. The mounds of poached animal parts confiscated by forest rangers reach almost to the ceiling. The air is stifling, the stench stomach-churning.

A problem

Ecologists worry that the construction of a natural gas pipeline in Russia's Ukok Plateau will destroy the habitat of endangered snow leopards, argali mountain sheep, and steppe eagles.

Conclude with strength

Use the ending paragraph to touch on your key points, but do not merely summarize. Leave your readers with something that will inspire them to continue to think about what you have written.

Issue a call to action

Although ecological problems in Russia seem distant, students like you and me can help protect the snow leopard by joining the World Wildlife Fund campaign.

Make recommendations

Russia's creditors would be wise to sign on to the World Wildlife Fund's proposal to relieve some of the country's debt in order to protect the snow leopard's habitat. After all, if Russia is going to be economically viable, it needs to be ecologically healthy.

Speculate about the future

Unless Nepali and Chinese officials devote more resources to snow leopard preservation, these beautiful animals will be gone in a few years.

6 Revise, Edit, and Proofread

The secret to writing well is rewriting.

6a Evaluate Your Draft

Use the following questions to evaluate your draft.

- Does your paper or project meet the assignment?
- Does your writing have a clear focus?
- Are your main points adequately developed?
- Can you rearrange sections or key points?
- Do you consider your readers' knowledge and points of view?
- Do you conclude emphatically?

When you finish, make a list of your goals for the revision.

6b Learn Strategies for Rewriting

1. **Keep your audience in mind.** Reread each paragraph's opening sentence and ask yourself whether the language is strong and engaging enough to keep your reader interested.
2. **Sharpen your focus wherever possible.** Revise your thesis and supporting paragraphs as needed. Check to see that your focus remains consistent throughout the essay.
3. **Check that key terms are adequately defined.** What are your key terms? Are they defined precisely enough to be meaningful?
4. **Develop where necessary.** Key points and claims may need more explanation and supporting evidence.
5. **Check links between paragraphs.** Underline the first and last sentences of each paragraph in your paper. Do these sentences together make a logical and coherent argument?

6. **Consider your title.** Be as specific as you can in your title, and, if possible, suggest your stance.
7. **Consider your introduction.** In the introduction you want to get off to a fast start and convince your reader to keep reading.
8. **Consider your conclusion.** Try to leave your reader with something interesting and provocative.

6c Edit For Specific Goals

1. **Check the connections between sentences.** If you need to signal a relationship between one sentence and the next, use a transitional word or phrase.
2. **Check your sentences.** If you noticed that a sentence was hard to read or didn't sound right when you read your paper aloud, think about how you might rephrase it.
3. **Eliminate wordiness.** See how many words you can take out without losing the meaning (see Chapter 19).
4. **Use active verbs.** Any time you can use a verb other than a form of *be* (*is, are, was, were*) or a verb ending in *-ing,* take advantage of the opportunity to make your style more lively (see Section 18b).
5. **Use specific and inclusive language.** As you read, stay alert for any vague words or phrases. Check to make sure that you have used inclusive language throughout (see Chapter 21).

6d Proofread Carefully

1. **Know what your spelling checker can and can't do.** Spelling checkers do not catch wrong words (e.g., "to much" should be "too much"), missing endings ("three dog"), and other, similar errors.
2. **Check for grammar and mechanics.** Nothing hurts your credibility with readers more than a text with numerous errors.

7 Write in Academic Genres

Learn to write in the many academic genres.

7a Write an Observation

Observations are common in the natural sciences and in social science disciplines such as psychology, sociology, and education. They begin as notes taken firsthand by the writer. Observations should include as many relevant and specific details as possible.

Elements of an observation

Title	Include a precise title.
Description and context	Be specific about what or whom you are observing. How did you limit your site or subject? What background information do readers need?
Record of observations	Report what you observed in some logical order: chronologically, from most obvious features to least obvious, or some other pattern.
Conclusion or summary	Give your readers a framework in which to understand your observations. What conclusions can you draw from them? What questions are left unanswered?

What you need to do

- Carry a notebook and make extensive field notes. Provide as much information as possible about the activities you observe.
- Record in your notebook exactly when you arrived and left, where you were, and exactly what you saw and heard.
- Analyze your observations before you write about them. Identify patterns, and organize your report according to those patterns.

Sample observation

Animal Activity in Barton Springs Pool
from 15 April to 22 April 2007

Barton Springs Pool is a 225-meter-long, natural spring-fed pool in a limestone creek bed in Austin, Texas. It is both a wildlife habitat and a busy hub of human activity. Because of the constant flow from the springs, the water temperature is constant at 68°F (20°C), allowing swimmers to use the pool year around.

Specific times, weather conditions, numbers of individual species, and behaviors are recorded.

My first observation was on 15 April from 1:45 p.m. to 4 p.m. on a warm sunny day with the air temperature at 74°F (23°C). I used a mask and snorkel to observe below the water. It was remarkable how oblivious people and wildlife were of each other. While from forty to fifty-five Austinites splashed on the surface, many fish (mostly smallmouth bass with two large channel catfish on the bottom) swam below them, and large numbers of crayfish crept along the rocky portion of the pool's bottom. Eight small turtles (red-eared sliders) alternately swam at the surface and dove below near the dam at the deep end. Twelve endangered Barton Springs salamanders (*Eurycea sosorum*), ranging in color from bright orange to paler yellow, were active by the larger spring at the center of the pool.

At the times when humans are not present or nearly absent, animal activity noticeably increases. From the side of the pool on 16 April (clear, 72°) from 7:25 p.m. until closing at 8 p.m., I observed smallmouth bass schooling near the dam and feeding on mosquitoes and mayflies. Nine ducks (seven lesser scaup and two mallards) landed on the pool at 7:40 p.m. and remained when I left. (Lesser scaup migrate to the area in large numbers in the winter; the mallards are likely domesticated ducks.) A pair of wood ducks (male and female) were also on the cliff above the shallow end.

7b Write a Case Study

Case studies are used in a wide range of fields such as nursing, psychology, business, and anthropology. Case studies are narrow in focus, providing a rich, detailed portrait of a specific event or subject.

Elements of a case study

Introduction	Explain the purpose of your study and how or why you selected your subject. Use language appropriate to your discipline, and specify the boundaries of your study.
Methodology	Explain the theories or formal process that guided your observations and analysis during the study.
Observations	Describe the "case" of the subject under study by writing a narrative, utilizing interviews, research, and other data to provide as much detail and specificity as possible.
Discussion	Explain how the variables in your case might interact. Don't generalize from your case to a larger context; stay within the limits of what you have observed.
Conclusion	What does all this information add up to? What is implied, suggested, or proven by your observations? What new questions arise?
References	Using the appropriate format, cite all the outside sources you have used. (See Chapter 15 for APA documentation and Chapter 17 for CSE documentation.)

What you need to do

- Understand the specific elements of your assignment. Ask your instructor about what your case study should include.
- Use careful observation and precise, detailed description to provide a complex picture with a narrow focus.
- Write your observations in the form of a narrative, placing yourself in the background (avoid using *I* or *me*).
- Analyze your findings and interpret their possible meanings, but draw your conclusions from the observed facts.

Sample case study

Underage Drinking Prevention Programs
in the Radisson School District

Introducion

This study examines the effect of Smith and Bingham's drinking-prevention curriculum on drinking rates in the Radisson School District, 2000-2006. Prior to 2002, the Radisson School District offered no formal drinking-prevention education. In 2000, as part of a state initiative, the district proposed several underage drinking education curricula for possible adoption. After substantial debate and input from parents, Smith and Bingham's curriculum was chosen for implementation in ninth through twelfth grades. This study tracks student drinking rates from 2000 to 2006 and compares the results after introduction of the curriculum to district rates prior to implementation.

Discussion

The data from this study showed no correlation between the curriculum and student drinking rates. Drinking rates remained unchanged before, during, and after the implementation of the curriculum. Additionally, survey data indicate that levels of student drinking remained constant as well. Therefore, Smith and Bingham's curriculum had minimal effect on changing students' drinking behavior.

Conclusion

In terms of reducing student drinking, Smith and Bingham's curriculum does not appear to be any more effective than no drinking-prevention education at all. Since no measurable results were obtained, the strong administrative support for the curriculum in the school district cannot be attributed to its success.

Some disciplines require title pages. See page 122 for an example of an APA title page.

The introduction identifies both the problem and the particular subject of the case study.

The conclusion sums up what has been observed. Many case studies do not give definitive answers but rather raise further questions to explore.

7c Write a Lab Report

Lab reports follow a strict structure, enabling specialists in a given field to assess quickly the experimental methods and findings in any report. Check with your instructor for the specific elements required for your lab report.

Elements of a lab report

Title	State exactly what was tested, using language specific to the field.
Abstract	Briefly state the questions and the findings in the report.
Introduction	Give the full context of the problem, defining the hypothesis being tested.
Methods	Describe the materials used as well as the method of investigation. Your methods and procedure sections should be specific enough to allow another researcher to replicate your experiment.
Procedure	Step by step, narrate exactly what you did and what happened. In most fields, you will use the passive voice.
Results	State the outcomes you obtained, providing carefully labeled charts and graphics as needed.
Discussion	State why you think you got the results you did, using your results to explain. If there were anomalies in your data, note them as well.
Conclusion	Briefly, what was learned from this experiment? What still needs to be investigated?
References	Using the appropriate format, cite all the outside sources you have used. (See Chapter 15 for pyschology lab reports and Chapter 17 for science lab reports.)

What you need to do

- Understand the question you are researching and the process you will use before you begin. Ask your instructor if you need clarification.

- Take thorough notes at each step of your process. You may be asked to keep a lab notebook with a specific format for recording data. Review your notes before you begin drafting your report.
- Don't get ahead of yourself. Keep methods, procedure, discussion, and conclusion sections separate. Remember that other scientists will look at specific sections of your report expecting to find certain kinds of information. If that information isn't where they expect it to be, your report will not make sense.
- Write your abstract last. Writing all the other sections of the report first will give you a much clearer picture of your findings.

Sample lab report

Wave interference in visible light using
the double-slit method

Abstract

Filtered light was projected through one slit in a piece of cardboard, producing a single bar of light, brightest in the center and shaded darker toward the edges, on the wall behind the cardboard. When a second slit was added to the cardboard, the projected image changed to alternating bands of bright light and darkness. The conclusion reached is that wavelength patterns in the light cancelled or reinforced one another as they reached the wall, increasing or decreasing the observed light. These results are consistent with the wave theory of light.

7d Write an Essay Exam

Instructors use essay exams to test your understanding of course concepts and to assess your ability to analyze ideas independently. To demonstrate these skills, you must write an essay that responds directly and fully to the question being asked.

Elements of an exam essay

Introduction	Briefly restate the question, summarizing the answer you will provide.
Body paragraphs	Each paragraph should address a major element of the question. Order them so the reader can tell how you are responding to the question. EXAMPLE Of the many factors leading to the downfall of Senator Joseph McCarthy, the Army-McCarthy hearings were the most important.
Conclusion	*Briefly* restate your answer to the question, not the question itself.

What you need to do

- Make sure you understand the question. Respond with the kinds of information and analysis the question asks you to provide.
- Plan your response before you begin writing, using an outline, list, or diagram. Note how much time you have to write your response.
- Address each element of the question, providing supporting evidence.
- Relate the point of each paragraph clearly to the larger argument.
- Save a few minutes to proofread and add information where needed.

PART 2

Researching

Five Steps for Planning and Conducting Research

Research is a creative process, which is another way of saying it is a messy process. Often there are false starts and dead ends. Even though the process is complex, your results will turn out better if you keep the big picture in mind.

1 How do I find a topic?

Look first at your assignment. For example, if the assignment asks for an argument, you will need to take a position on an issue.

- Look at your class notes and the readings for your course for possible topics.
- Browse a Web subject directory such as Yahoo! Directory (dir.yahoo.com) or the Library of Congress Virtual Reference Shelf (www.loc.gov/rr/askalib/virtualref.html).
- Browse an online encyclopedia such as the *Columbia Encyclopedia* (www.bartleby.com/65/) or Britannica Online (www. britannica.com). Your library's Web site has other resources listed by subject.

2 How do I focus a topic and draft a thesis?

It can be tricky to find a balance between what you want to say about a topic and the amount of space you have to say it in. Usually your instructor will suggest a length for your paper, which should help you decide how to limit your topic. If you suspect your topic is becoming unmanageable, and your paper may be too long, look for ways to narrow the focus of your research.

Think of questions related to your topic, and use your answers to those questions to formulate a specific thesis.

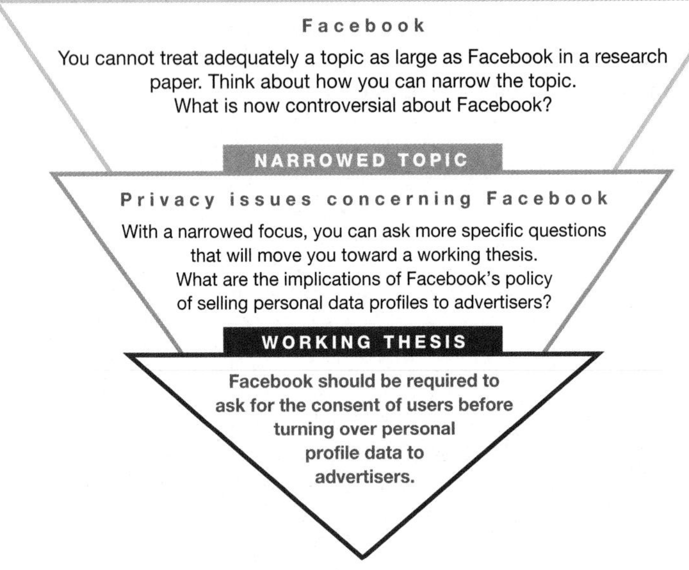

3 How do I determine what kind of research I need?

Ask these questions before you start your research.

- How much information do you need? The assignment may specify the number of sources you should consult.
- Are particular types of sources—such as books, scholarly journals, or government statistics—required?
- How current should the information be? Some topics, such as privacy issues concerning Facebook, may require you to use the most up-to-date information you can locate.
- Do you need to consider point of view? Argument assignments sometimes require you to consider opposing viewpoints on an issue.
- Do you need to do field research? For example, if you are researching a campus issue such as the problem of inadequate parking for students, you may need to conduct interviews, make observations, and take a survey (see Chapter 12).

4 How do I find sources?

Most people who do research rely partly or exclusively on the work of others as sources of information. If you are unsure where to start, visit your library and talk to a research librarian.

Source	Type of Information	How to Find Them
Scholarly books (see Chapter 10)	Extensive and in-depth coverage of nearly any subject	Library catalog
Scholarly journals (see Chapter 8)	Reports of new knowledge and research findings by experts	Online library databases
Newspapers and magazines (see Chapter 8)	Recent and current information	Online library databases
Government publications (see Chapter 9)	Government-collected statistics, studies, and reports; especially good for science and medicine	Library catalog and city, state, and federal government Web sites
Videos, audios, documentaries, maps (see Chapter 9)	Information varies widely	Library catalog, Web, and online library databases

5 How do I keep track of my research?

As you begin to collect your sources, make sure you get full bibliographic information for everything you might want to use in your project: articles, books, Web sites, and other materials. Decide which documentation style you will use. If your instructor does not tell you which style is appropriate, ask. (The major documentation styles—MLA, APA, Chicago (CMS), and CSE—are dealt with in detail in Chapters 14–17.)

You can record bibliographic information in different ways: by using notecards, by printing out or photocopying sources, by e-mailing articles to yourself from your library's databases, or by using your library's software for managing citations. Always check that you have complete and accurate information.

8 Find Sources in Databases

Library databases combine convenience with the reliability of a library.

8a Know the Strengths of Database Sources

Sources found through library databases have already been filtered for you by trained librarians. They will include some common sources like popular magazines and newspapers, but the greatest value of database sources are the many journals, abstracts, studies, and other sources produced by specialists whose work has been scrutinized and commented upon by other experts.

Know the advantages of library database sources versus Web sources

	Library database sources	Web sources
Speed	✓ Users can find information quickly	✓ Users can find information quickly
Accessibility	✓ Available 24/7	✓ Available 24/7
Organization	✓ Materials are organized for efficient search and retrieval	Users must look in many different places for information
Consistency and quality	✓ Librarians review and select resources	Anyone can claim to be an "expert," regardless of qualifications
Comprehensiveness	✓ Collected sources represent a wide body of knowledge	No guarantee that the full breadth of an issue will be represented
Permanence	✓ Materials remain available for many years	Materials can disappear or change in an instant

Free of overt bias	✓ Sources are required to meet certain standards of documentation and rigor	Sources are often a soapbox for organizations or individuals with particular agendas
Free of commercial slant	✓ Sources are largely commercial-free	Sources often try to sell you something

8b Find Information in Databases

You must first locate databases in order to use them. Usually you can find them on your library's Web site. Sometimes databases are listed in alphabetical order. Sometimes you select a subject, and then you are directed to databases. Sometimes you select the name of a database vendor such as EBSCO, FirstSearch, or Ovid. The vendor is the company that provides databases to the library.

It can be confusing to determine the name of the database and the name of the vendor, but you will need to understand this distinction in order to document your research. LexisNexis, for example, is both the name of the database and the name of the vendor. In contrast, Academic Search Premier and Academic Search Complete are databases offered by EBSCO, and in some libraries you click on EBSCOhost to get to Academic Search Premier or Academic Search Complete.

You can learn how to use databases in your library with the help of a reference librarian. Your library may also have online and printed tutorials on using databases.

8c Construct Effective Database Searches

To use databases effectively, make a list of keywords in advance. Keywords might come from your researchable question or your working thesis. You will need keywords to search in a database. For example, a search for voter participation trends among young adults might begin with the terms **young adult** and **voters**. You will probably want to focus on the most recent information you can find. It's important to know if voter participation among young adults is increasing or decreasing, for example.

LEARN THE ART OF EFFECTIVE KEYWORD SEARCHES

Keyword searching of databases is similar to using search engines for the Web (see Chapter 9) and for your library's online catalog subject index (see Chapter 10).

Use two methods to generate your list of possible keywords. First, think of keywords that make your search **more specific**. For example, a search for sources related to youth voter participation might focus more specifically on "young adults" and

- voter registration
- party affiliation
- historical participation rates
- voter turnout

Also think about **more general** ways to describe what you are doing—what synonyms can you think of for your existing terms? Other people may have discussed the topic using those terms instead. Instead of relying on "young adult," you can also try keywords like

- youth
- under 30
- Generation Y
- college students

Many databases have a thesaurus that can help you find more keywords.

Your next step is to choose a database to begin your research. To research voter participation among young adults, you'll need to access newspapers,

popular journals, and scholarly journals. You'll need to use a general database such as Academic OneFile, Academic Search Premier, Academic Search Complete, or LexisNexis Academic.

8d Locate Elements of a Citation in Database Sources

Sometimes you will find exactly what you are looking for by using a database, but then you may become frustrated when you cannot find it again. It's critical to keep track of how you get to particular articles and other materials—both to find them again and to cite each item in your list of works cited.

You must document information you get from database sources just as for print sources. The reason you document sources is to allow your readers to view exactly the same sources you looked at.

Figure 8.1 (on the following page) shows an article from the LexisNexis Academic search for *privacy Facebook.* To cite this article in MLA style, you'll need the following information.

Author's name	Rampell, Catherine
Title of article	"What Facebook Knows That You Don't"
Publication information	
Name of newspaper	*Washington Post*
Date of publication (and edition for newspapers)	23 Feb. 2008, regional ed.
Section and page number	A15
Database information	
Name of database	*LexisNexis Academic*
Date you accessed the site	28 Apr. 2009

For any sources you find on databases, MLA style requires you to provide the full print information, the name of the database in italics, the medium of publication (*Web*), and the date you accessed the database. If page numbers are not included, use *n. pag.* Do *not* include the URL of the database.

The citation for the article in Figure 8.1 would appear as follows in an MLA-style works-cited list (see Section 14f).

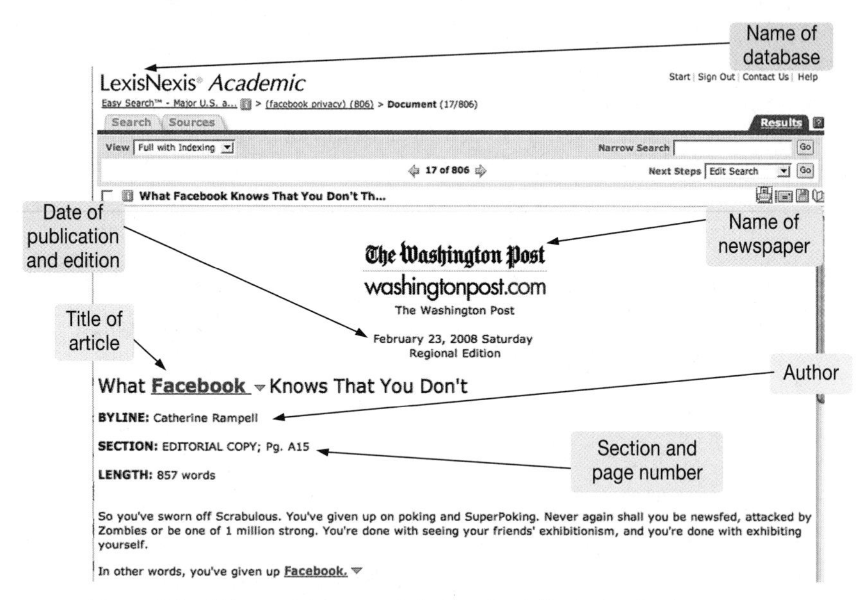

Figure 8.1 Citing a database article from LexisNexis Academic

> Rampell, Catherine. "What Facebook Knows That You Don't." *Washington Post* 22 Feb. 2008, regional ed.: A15. *LexisNexis Academic*. Web. 28 Apr. 2009.

APA style no longer requires listing the names of common databases or listing the date of access, unless the content is likely to change. If you name the database, do not list the URL. Here's how the citation for the article in Figure 8.1 would appear in an APA-style references list (see Section 15d).

Rampell, C. (2008, February 23). What Facebook knows that you don't. *The Washington Post*, p. A15. Retrieved from LexisNexis Academic database.

Many scholarly publishers now use a Digital Object Identifier (DOI), a unique alphanumeric string that is permanent. If you can find a DOI, list it at the end of the APA-style entry.

9 Find Sources on the Web

The Web has many traps for unwary researchers.

9a Find Reliable Web Sources

The Web offers you some resources for current topics that would be difficult or impossible to find in a library. The key to successful research is knowing where to find current, accurate, and high-quality information about the particular question you are researching.

Search engines

Search engines designed for the Web work in ways similar to library databases and your library's online catalog—with one major difference. Databases typically do some screening of the items they list, but search engines take you to potentially everything on the Web—millions of pages in all.

Consequently, you have to work harder to limit searches on the Web; otherwise you will be deluged.

There are three basic kinds of search engines.

1. **Keyword search engines** (e.g., Ask.com, Google, MSN, Yahoo!). Keyword search engines give different results because they assign different weights to the information they find.
2. **Web directories** (e.g., Britannica.com, Yahoo! Directory). Web directories classify Web sites into categories and are the closest equivalent to the cataloging system used by libraries.
3. **Specialized search engines.** Specialized search engines include
   - regional search engines (e.g., Baidu for China)
   - medical search engines (e.g., WebMD)
   - legal search engines (e.g., Lexis)
   - job search engines (e.g., Monster.com)
   - property search engines (e.g., Zillow)
   - comparison-shopping search engines (e.g., Froogle)

No doubt we'll see many more specialized search engines develop.

Online government sources

The federal and state governments have made many of their publications available on the Web. Often the most current and most reliable statistics are government statistics. Among the more important government resources are the following:

- **Bureau of Labor Statistics** (www.bls.gov/). Source for official U.S. government statistics on employment, wages, and consumer prices.
- **Census Bureau** (www.census.gov/). Contains a wealth of links to sites for population, social, economic, and political statistics, including the *Statistical Abstract of the United States* (www.census.gov/compendia/statab/).
- **Centers for Disease Control** (www.cdc.gov/). Authoritative and trustworthy source for health statistics.

- **CIA World Factbook** (www.cia.gov/library/publications/the-world-factbook/). Resource for geographic, economic, demographic, and political information on the nations of the world.
- **Library of Congress** (www.loc.gov/). Many of the resources of the largest library in the world are available on the Web.
- **National Institutes of Health** (www.nih.gov/). Extensive health information, including MedlinePlus searches.
- **THOMAS** (thomas.loc.gov/). The major source of legislative information, including bills, committee reports, and voting records of individual members of Congress.
- **USA.gov** (www.usa.gov/). The place to start when you are not sure where to look for government information.

Search blogs

Blogs began as online diaries in the 1990s; since then they have moved closer to mainstream media and are now published by politicians, political consultants, news editors, and various experts. Specialized search engines allow you to find subjects discussed in blogs.

- **Bloglines** (www.bloglines.com). Searches blogs and Internet forums.
- **Google Blog Search** (blogsearch.google.com). Searches blogs in several languages besides English.
- **IceRocket** (blogs.icerocket.com). Searches blogs and MySpace.
- **Technorati** (www.technorati.com). Searches blogs and other user-generated content.

Search for visual sources

Three major search engines are designed specifically to find images:

- **Google Image Search** (images.google.com). The most comprehensive image search tool.
- **Picsearch** (www.picsearch.com). Provides thumbnails of images linked to the source on the Web.
- **Yahoo! Search** (images.search.yahoo.com). Has tools to limit results on the Advanced Search similar to Google.

KNOW THE LIMITATIONS OF WIKIPEDIA

Wikipedia is a valuable resource for popular culture topics that are not covered in traditional encyclopedias. You can find out SpongeBob SquarePants's original name ("SpongeBoy," but it had already been copyrighted), how many home runs Sammy Sosa hit in 1998 (66; Mark McGwire hit 70 the same year), whether David Lee Roth or Sammy Hagar was the lead singer on Van Halen's "Finish What Ya Started" (Hagar), and which years the Red Hot Chili Peppers were the headliners at Coachella (2003 and 2007).

Wikipedia, however, is not considered a reliable source of information for a research paper by many instructors and the scholarly community in general. The problem with Wikipedia is that anyone can change an entry, and there are too many anonymous abusers. Wikipedia had to tighten its rules in 2005 after a journalist complained that his biography on Wikipedia claimed for four months that he was suspected in the assassinations of John F. Kennedy and Robert F. Kennedy.

Even with steps to correct some of the worst problems, too much erroneous information remains on Wikipedia. To be on the safe side, treat Wikipedia as you would a blog. It can be a source of ideas, but you'll need to confirm in a reliable source any facts you want to include in your research.

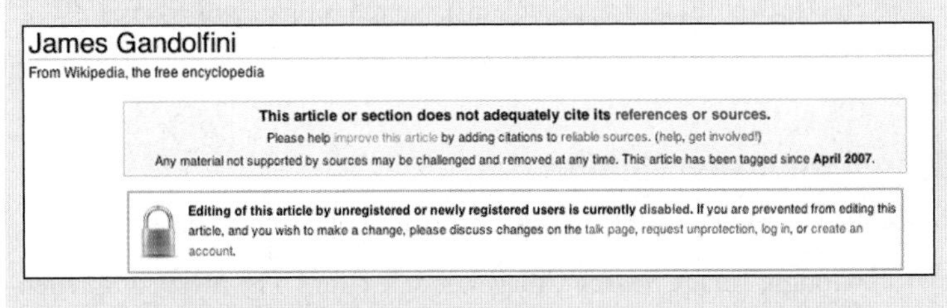
James Gandolfini

From Wikipedia, the free encyclopedia

This article or section does not adequately cite its references or sources.
Please help improve this article by adding citations to reliable sources. (help, get involved!)
Any material not supported by sources may be challenged and removed at any time. This article has been tagged since **April 2007**.

Editing of this article by unregistered or newly registered users is currently disabled. If you are prevented from editing this article, and you wish to make a change, please discuss changes on the talk page, request unprotection, log in, or create an account.

Wikipedia now attaches warning labels to articles that are incomplete, lack sources, or may contain mistakes.

9b Construct Effective Web Searches

Subject searches require keywords, so it's important to start your search with a good list of keywords. See the box on page 30 for advice on generating keywords.

As you look through your initial search results, keep the following facts in mind.

- Results that come up at the top of a list aren't necessarily the best sources—and the sequence or apparent ranking is not explained.
- Search engines often return some results that are advertisements.
- Search engines rank results in different ways based on factors such as the match with your keywords, the current popularity of a particular Web page, and the total traffic at the site hosting the page.

KNOW HOW TO USE GOOGLE AND OTHER SEARCH ENGINES EFFECTIVELY

Search engines often produce too many hits. If you look only at the first few items, you may miss what is most valuable. Use the **advance search option** to refine your search.

The advanced searches on Google and Yahoo! give you the options of using a string of words to search for sites that contain (1) all the words, (2) the exact phrase, (3) any of the words, (4) without certain words. They also allow you to specify the language of the site, the date range, the file format, and the domain. For example, if you want to limit a search for multiple sclerosis to government Web sites such as the National Institutes of Health, you can specify the domain as **.gov**.

9c Locate Elements of a Citation in Web Sources

As you conduct your online research, make sure you collect the necessary bibliographic information for everything you might want to use as a source. Depending on the citation format you use, you'll arrange this information in a specific order.

Collect the following information about a Web site. The example below is an article in a magazine published on the Web.

Author's name, if available (if not, use the associated institution or organization)	Brooks, Kim
Title of article	"Slave to the Boob Tube"
Publication information	
Name of site or online journal	*Salon.com*
Sponsoring organization if available (for MLA)	Salon
Date of publication (for an article) or of site's last update	17 Mar. 2008
Date you accessed the site	2 Apr. 2009
URL (for APA)	http://www.salon.com/mwt/feature/2008/03/17/babies_and_tv/print.html

For example, if you are doing research on the effects of television on infants, you might cite the article shown in Figure 9.1, which discusses current research and gives a more personal account of the difficulties of preventing children from watching television.

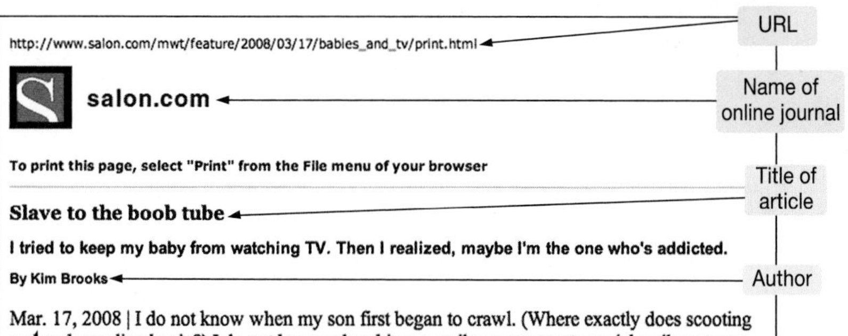
http://www.salon.com/mwt/feature/2008/03/17/babies_and_tv/print.html

salon.com

To print this page, select "Print" from the File menu of your browser

Slave to the boob tube

I tried to keep my baby from watching TV. Then I realized, maybe I'm the one who's addicted.

By Kim Brooks

Mar. 17, 2008 | I do not know when my son first began to crawl. (Where exactly does scooting end and crawling begin?) I do not know when his gas smiles gave way to social smiles or even [illegible]n he held his first bottle. Most of his milestones have been fairly ambiguous events. But the [illegible]ime he watched television was impossible to miss.

Figure 9.1 Highlighted is all the information you need to cite a Web source. This information appears in different places on different sites and sometimes is missing.

MLA works-cited entries no longer require listing the URL except when the URL is necessary to find the item.

Brooks, Kim. "Slave to the Boob Tube." *Salon.com*. Salon, 17 Mar. 2007. Web. 2 Apr. 2009.

APA style requires listing the URL but not the date of access.

Brooks, K. (2008, March 17). Slave to the boob tube. *Salon.com*. Retrieved from http://www.salon.com/mwt/feature/2008/03/17/babies_and_tv/print.html

You will find more examples of how to cite Web sources in MLA style in Section 14e and APA style in Section 15e.

10 Find Print Sources

Your professional librarian can help you locate sources.

10a Know the Strengths of Print Sources

No matter how current the topic you are researching, you will likely find information in print sources that is simply not available online. Print sources also have other advantages.

- They are arranged according to subject.
- Their individual contents are often indexed, and they may be listed in table form at the beginning of the work.
- They can be searched for in multiple ways—such as author, title, subject, and call letter.
- The majority of print sources have been evaluated by scholars, editors, and publishers, who determined that they merited publication.
- Print sources in your library have also been evaluated by trained librarians, whose job is to get the best and most useful research tools.

10b Find Books

Scholarly books offer you in-depth analyses of many subjects. They also contain bibliographies that can help you find other resources on a particular subject. You can find books by using your library's catalog and conducting a subject search.

For example, a subject search for "obesity" AND "children" might turn up the following record in your library.

Author, title, and publication information

Author	Ellin, Abby
Title	Teenage waistland: a former fat kid weighs in on living large, losing weight, and how parents can (and can't) help
Published	New York: Public Affairs, 2005.
Description	xli, 257 p.; 25 cm.
Notes	Includes bibliographical references (p. 223-248) and index.
Subjects	Ellin, Abby Overweight children—United States—Biography. Obesity in children—Treatment. Camps for overweight children. Child rearing
ISBN	1586482289
OCLC NUMBER	58422627
Call Number and Library for item location	RJ 399 C6 E387 2005 Main Library Stacks

Subject terms can help you find other books on the same topic

Call number and location

10c Find Journal Articles

Like books, scholarly journals provide in-depth examinations of subjects. The articles in scholarly journals are written by experts, and they usually contain lists of references that can guide you to other research on a subject. Articles in popular magazines are typically written by journalists. Some instructors frown on using popular magazines, but these journals can be valuable for researching current opinion on a particular topic.

Indexes for scholarly journals and magazines are available on your library's Web site (see Chapter 8 for in-depth advice on database searching). Databases increasingly contain the full text of articles, allowing you to read and copy the contents onto your computer.

10d Locate Elements of a Citation in Print Sources

As you begin to collect your sources, make sure you get full bibliographic information for everything you might want to use in your project. (The major documentation styles—MLA, APA, CMS, and CSE—are dealt with in detail in Chapters 14–17.)

For books, you will need at minimum the following information, which can typically be found on the front and back of the title page.

Author's name	Ojito, Mirta
Title of the book	*Finding Manaña: A Memoir of a Cuban Exile*
Publication information	
Place of publication	New York
Name of publisher	Penguin
Date of publication	2005
Medium of publication	Print

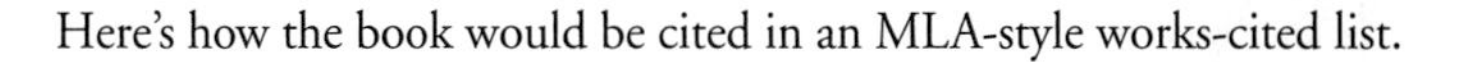

Here's how the book would be cited in an MLA-style works-cited list.

Ojito, Mirta. *Finding Manaña: A Memoir of a Cuban Exile*. New York: Penguin, 2005. Print.

Here's the APA citation for the same book.

Ojito, M. (2005). *Finding manaña: A memoir of a Cuban exile*. New York: Penguin.

For scholarly journals you will need the following.

Author's name	Longaker, Mark Garrett
Title of article	"Idealism and Early-American Rhetoric"
Publication information	
Name of journal	*Rhetoric Society Quarterly*
Volume number and issue number	36.3
Date of publication (and edition for newspapers)	2006
Page numbers of the article	281-308
Medium of publication	Print

An entry in an MLA-style works-cited list would look like this:

Longaker, Mark Garrett. "Idealism and Early-American Rhetoric." *Rhetoric Society Quarterly* 36.3 (2006): 281-308. Print.

And in APA style, like this:

Longaker, M. G. (2006). Idealism and early-American rhetoric. *Rhetoric Society Quarterly, 36*, 281–308.

11 Evaluate Your Sources

Becoming a successful researcher requires you to evaluate all sources you find.

11a Determine the Relevance of Sources

Whether you use print or online sources, a successful search will turn up many more items than you can expect to use in your final product. Use your working thesis to determine which sources are relevant to your project.

For example, if your research question asks why the Roman Empire declined rapidly at the end of the fourth and beginning of the fifth centuries AD, you may find older sources as valuable as new ones. Edward Gibbon's three-volume history, *The Decline and Fall of the Roman Empire*, remains an important source even though it was published in 1776 and 1781. But if you ask a research question about contemporary events—for example, the opposition to surveillance cameras for enforcing traffic laws—you will need the most current information you can find. You will want to learn why citizens vigorously oppose the cameras and why they are now illegal in nine states.

GUIDELINES FOR DETERMINING THE RELEVANCE OF SOURCES

- Does a source you have found address your research question?
- Is the information specialized enough for your needs?
- Is the information detailed enough for your needs?
- Does a source support or disagree with your working thesis? (You should not throw out work that challenges your views.)
- Does a source add to your content in an important way?
- Is the material you have found persuasive?
- What indications of possible bias do you note in the source?

11b Determine the Quality of Print and Database Sources

Database sources will be more pertinent to your research than general Web sources, and you can generally depend on them to be reliable, but you still have to evaluate them.

GUIDELINES FOR EVALUATING PRINT AND DATABASE SOURCES

- **Who wrote the source?** What are the author's qualifications? What organization does he or she represent?
- **Who published the source?** Scholarly books and articles in scholarly journals are reviewed by experts in the field before they are published. They are generally more reliable than popular magazines and books, which tend to emphasize what is sensational or entertaining at the expense of accuracy and comprehensiveness.
- **How current is the source?** If you are researching a fast-developing subject such as changes in breast cancer rates, then currency is important.
- **Where does the evidence in the source come from?** Is it from other sources, interviews, observations, surveys, or experiments? Is the evidence adequate to support the author's claims?
- **Can you detect particular biases of the author?** How do the author's biases affect the interpretation offered?

11c Determine the Quality of Web Sources

Always approach Web sites with an eye toward evaluating their content. No one is banned from the Web, no matter what a person's opinions or motives may be. Thus it's no surprise that much of what is on the Web is highly opinionated or false (or both).

Some Web sites are put up as jokes. Other Web sites are deliberately misleading. Many prominent Web sites draw imitators who want to cash in on the commercial visibility. The Web site for the Campaign for Tobacco-Free Kids (www.tobaccofreekids.org), for example, has an imitator (www.smokefreekids.com) that sells software for antismoking education. The .com URL is often a tip-off that a site has a profit motive.

GUIDELINES FOR EVALUATING WEB SOURCES

- **Are you viewing an entire Web site or just part of one?** Often search engines take you deep within a site with many pages. Look for a link to the main page.
- **What organization sponsors the Web site?** When a Web site doesn't indicate ownership, then you have to make judgments about who put it up and why.
- **Where does the information come from?** Does the Web site list the sources of facts or statistics?
- **Is the author of the Web site identified?** Be cautious about information on an anonymous site.
- **What are the author's or organization's qualifications to write about this topic?** If you cannot find this information on the Web site, use a search engine to learn more about the person or organization.
- **Is the information on the Web site current?** Many Web pages do not list when they were last updated; thus, you cannot determine their currency.
- **Is the author objective?** Many Web sites try to persuade you to take a particular point of view.
- **Is the Web site trying to sell you something?** Many Web sites are no more trustworthy than other forms of advertising.

12 Plan Field Research

Gather information through interviews, surveys, and observations.

12a Know What You Can Obtain from Field Research

Even though much of the research you do for college courses will be secondary research conducted at a computer or in the library, some topics do call for primary research, requiring you to gather information on your own. Field research of this kind can be especially important for exploring local issues.

Be aware that the ethics of conducting field research require you to inform people about what you are doing and why you are gathering information. If you are uncertain about the ethics of doing field research, talk to your instructor.

Three types of field research that can usually be conducted in college are interviews, surveys, and observations.

- **Interviews**: Interviewing experts on your research topic can help build your knowledge base. You can also use interviews to discover what the people most affected by a particular issue are thinking and feeling.
- **Surveys**: Small surveys can often provide insight on local issues.
- **Observations**: Local observations can also be a valuable source of data. For example, if you are researching why a particular office on your campus does not operate efficiently, you might observe what happens when students enter.

12b Conduct Interviews

Before you contact anyone to ask for an interview, think carefully about your goals; knowing what you want to find out through your interviews will help you determine whom you need to interview and what questions you need to ask.

- Decide what you want or need to know and who best can provide that information for you.
- Schedule each interview in advance, and let the person know why you are conducting the interview.
- Plan your questions in advance. Write down a few questions and have a few more in mind. Listen carefully so you can follow up on key points.
- Come prepared with a notebook and pencil for taking notes and jotting down short quotations. Record the date, time, place, and subject of the interview. If you want to use a tape recorder, ask for permission in advance.
- When you are finished, thank your subject and ask his or her permission to get in touch again if you have additional questions.
- When you are ready to incorporate the interview into a paper or project, think about what you want to highlight about the interview and which direct quotations to include.

12c Administer Surveys

Use surveys to find out what groups of people think about a topic. You need to decide what exactly you want to know, then design a survey that will provide that information.

- Write specific questions. To make sure your questions are clear, test them on a few people before you conduct the survey.
- Include one or two open-ended questions, such as "What do you like about X?" "What don't you like about X?" Open-ended questions can be difficult to interpret, but sometimes they turn up information you had not anticipated.

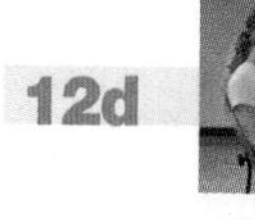

- Decide whom and how many people you will need to survey. For example, if you want to claim that the results of your survey represent the views of residents of a dormitory, your method of selecting respondents should give all residents an equal chance to be selected. Don't select only your friends.
- Decide how you will contact participants in your survey. If you are going to mail or e-mail your survey, include a statement about what the survey is for and a deadline for returning it.
- Think about how you will interpret your survey. Multiple-choice formats make data easy to tabulate, but often they miss key information. Open-ended questions will require you to figure out a way to group responses.
- When writing about the results, be sure to include information about who participated in the survey, how the participants were selected, and when and how the survey was administered.

12d Make Observations

Observing what goes on in a place can be an effective research tool. Your observations can inform a controversy or topic by providing a vivid picture of real-world activity.

- Choose a place where you can observe with the least intrusion. The less people wonder about what you are doing, the better.
- Carry a notebook and write extensive field notes. Get down as much information as you can, and worry about analyzing it later.
- Record the date, exactly where you were, exactly when you arrived and left, and important details such as the number of people present.
- Write on one side of your notebook so you can use the facing page to note key observations and analyze your data later.

13 Incorporate Sources and Avoid Plagiarism

Build on the research of others by using sources accurately and fairly.

13a Avoid Plagiarism

You know that copying someone else's paper word for word or taking an article off the Internet and turning it in as yours is **plagiarism**. But if plagiarism also means using the ideas, melodies, or images of someone else without acknowledging them, then the concept is much broader and more difficult to define.

What you don't have to document

Fortunately, common sense governs issues of academic plagiarism. The standards of documentation are not so strict that the source of every fact you cite must be acknowledged. Suppose you are writing about the causes of maritime disasters and you want to know how many people drowned when the *Titanic* sank on the early morning of April 15, 1912. You check the *Britannica Online* Web site and find that the death toll was around 1,500. Since this fact is available in many reference works, you would not need to cite *Britannica Online* as the source.

What you do have to document

For facts that are not easily found in general reference works, statements of opinion, and arguable claims, you must cite the source. You must also cite the sources of statistics, research findings, examples, graphs, charts, and illustrations. When in doubt, always document the source.

COMMON ERRORS

Plagiarism in college writing

If you find any of the following problems in your academic writing, it is likely you are plagiarizing someone else's work. Because plagiarism is usually inadvertent, it is especially important that you understand what constitutes using sources responsibly.

- **Missing attribution**. The author of a quotation has not been identified. A lead-in or signal phrase that provides attribution to the source is not used, and no author is identified in the citation.
- **Missing quotation marks.** Quotation marks do not appear around material quoted directly from a source.
- **Inadequate citation.** No page number is given to show where in the source the quotation, paraphrase, or summary is drawn from.
- **Paraphrase relies too heavily on the source.** Either the wording or sentence structure of a paraphrase follows the source too closely.
- **Distortion of meaning.** A paraphrase or summary distorts the meaning of the source, or a quotation is taken out of context, resulting in a change of meaning.
- **Missing Works Cited entry.** The Works Cited page does not include all the works cited in the paper.
- **Inadequate citation of images.** A figure or photo appears with no label, number, caption, or citation to indicate the source of the image. If material includes a summary of data from a visual source, no attribution or citation is given for the graph being summarized.

13b Quote Sources Without Plagiarizing

Most people who get into plagiarism trouble lift words from a source and use them without quotation marks. Where the line is drawn is easiest to illustrate with an example. In the following passage, Steven Johnson takes issue with the metaphor of surfing applied to the Web:

> Web surfing and channel surfing are genuinely different pursuits; to imagine them as equivalents is to ignore the defining characteristics of each medium. . . . A channel surfer hops back and forth between different channels because she's bored. A Web surfer clicks on a link because she's interested.
>
> —Johnson, Steven. *Interface Culture: How New Technology Transforms the Way We Create and Communicate.* New York: Harper, 1997. 107-09.

If you were writing a paper or putting up a Web site that concerned Web surfing, you might want to mention the distinction that Johnson makes between channel surfing and surfing the Web. Your options are to paraphrase the source or to quote it directly.

If you quote directly, you must place quotation marks around all words you take from the original:

> One observer marks this contrast: "A channel surfer hops back and forth between different channels because she's bored. A Web surfer clicks on a link because she's interested" (Johnson 109).

Notice that the quotation is introduced and not just dropped in. This example follows Modern Language Association (MLA) style, where the citation goes outside the quotation marks but before the final period.

13c Summarize and Paraphrase Sources Without Plagiarizing

Summarize

When you *summarize,* you state the major ideas of an entire source or part of a source in a paragraph or perhaps even a sentence. The key is to put the

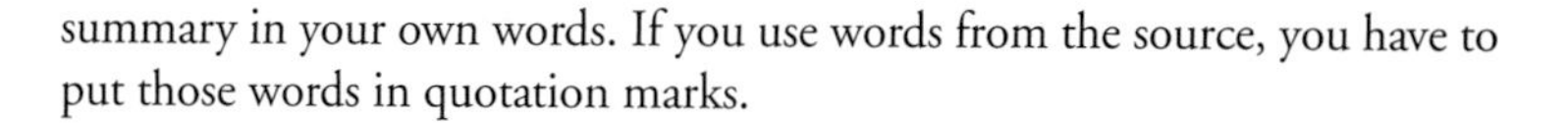

summary in your own words. If you use words from the source, you have to put those words in quotation marks.

Plagiarized

> Steven Johnson argues in *Interface Culture* that the concept of "surfing" is misapplied to the Internet because **channel surfers hop back and forth between different channels because** they're **bored**, but **Web surfers click on links because** they're **interested.**

> [Most of the words are lifted directly from the original.]

Acceptable Summary

> Steven Johnson argues in *Interface Culture* that the concept of "surfing" is misapplied to the Internet because users of the Web consciously choose to link to other sites while television viewers mindlessly flip through the channels until something catches their attention.

Paraphrase

When you *paraphrase,* you represent the idea of the source in your own words at about the same length as the original. You still need to include the reference to the source of the idea. The following example illustrates what is not an acceptable paraphrase.

Plagiarized

> Steven Johnson argues that the concept of "surfing" does a terrible injustice to what it means to navigate around the Web. Surfing is not a bad metaphor for channel hopping, but it doesn't fit what people do on the Web. **Web surfing and channel surfing** are truly **different** activities; **to imagine them as** the same **is to ignore** their **defining characteristics. A channel surfer** skips around **because she's bored** while a **Web surfer clicks on a link because she's interested** (107-09).

Even though the source is listed, this paraphrase is unacceptable. Too many of the words in the original are repeated here. When a string of words is lifted from a source and inserted without quotation marks, the passage is plagiarized.

A true paraphrase represents an entire rewriting of the idea from the source.

Acceptable Paraphrase

> Steven Johnson argues that "surfing" is a misleading term for describing how people navigate on the Web. He allows that "surfing" is appropriate for clicking across television channels because the viewer has to interact with what the networks and cable companies provide, just as the surfer has to interact with what the ocean provides. Web surfing, according to Johnson, operates at much greater depth and with much more consciousness of purpose. Web surfers actively follow links to make connections (107-09).

Even though there are a few words from the original in this paraphrase, such as *navigate* and *connections*, these sentences are original in structure and wording while accurately conveying the meaning of the source.

13d Incorporate Quotations, Summaries, and Paraphrases Effectively

The purpose of using sources is to *support* what you have to say, not to say something for you. Next to plagiarism, the worst mistake you can make with sources is to string together a series of long quotations. If you want to refer to an idea or fact and the original wording is not critical, make the point in your own words. Save direct quotations for language that is memorable or gives the character of the source.

Block quotations

If a direct quotation is long, it is indented from the margin instead of being placed in quotation marks. In MLA style, a quotation longer than four lines should be indented one inch or ten spaces. A quotation of forty words or longer is indented one-half inch or five spaces in APA style. In both MLA and APA styles, long quotations are double-spaced. When you indent a long quotation

in this way, it is called a **block quotation**. You still need to integrate a block quotation into the text of your paper. Block quotations should be introduced by mentioning where they came from. Note three points about form in the block quotation.

- There are no quotation marks around the block quotation.
- Words quoted in the original retain the double quotation marks.
- The page number appears after the period at the end of the block quotation.

It is a good idea to include at least one or two sentences following the quotation to describe its significance to your thesis.

Integrate quotations, summaries, and paraphrases

You should check to see whether all sources are well integrated into the fabric of your paper. Introduce quotations by attributing them in the text:

> Many soldiers who fought for the United States in the U.S.-Mexican War of 1846 were skeptical of American motives, including Civil War hero and future president Ulysses S. Grant, who wrote: "We were sent to provoke a fight, but it was essential that Mexico should commence it" (68).

Summaries and paraphrases likewise need introductions. In the following summary, signal phrases make it clear which ideas come from the source. The summary also indicates the stance of Lewis and includes a short quotation that gives the flavor of the source.

> In 2001 it became as fashionable to say the Internet changes nothing as it had been to claim the Internet changes everything just two years before. In the midst of the Internet gloom, one prominent contrarian has emerged to defend the Internet. Michael Lewis observes in *Next: The Future Just Happened* that it's as if "some crusty old baron who had been blasted out of his castle and was finally having a look at his first cannon had said, 'All it does is speed up balls'" (14). Lewis claims that while the profit-making potential of the Internet was overrated, the social effects were not. He sees the Internet demolishing old castles of expertise along with many traditional relationships based on that expertise.

USE QUOTATIONS EFFECTIVELY

Quotations are a frequent problem area in research papers. Review every quotation to ensure that each is used effectively and correctly.

- **Limit the use of long quotations.** If you have more than one block quotation on a page, look closely to see if one or more of them can be paraphrased or summarized.
- **Check that each quotation supports your major points rather than making major points for you.** A common mistake is to drop in quotations without introducing them or indicating their significance.
- **Check that each quotation is introduced and attributed.** Each quotation should be introduced and its author or title named.
- **Check for verbs that signal a quotation:** Smith *claims,* Jones *argues,* Brown *states.* Use a signal verb that suggests how you are using a source. For example, if you write "McNeil contends," your reader is alerted that you are likely to disagree with your source.
- **Check that each quotation is properly formatted and punctuated.** Prose quotations longer than four lines (MLA) or forty words (APA) should be indented ten spaces in MLA style or five spaces in APA style. Shorter quotations should be enclosed within quotation marks.
- **Check that you cite the source for each quotation.** You are required to cite the sources of all direct quotations, paraphrases, and summaries.
- **Check the accuracy of each quotation.** It's easy to leave out words or mistype a quotation. Compare what is in your paper to the original source. If you need to add words to make a quotation grammatical, make sure the added words are in brackets. Use ellipses to indicate omitted words.
- **Read your paper aloud to a classmate or a friend.** Each quotation should flow smoothly when you read your paper aloud. Put a check beside rough spots as you read aloud so you can revise later.

PART 3

Documentation

Five Steps for Documenting Sources

1 Which documentation style do I use?

Different disciplines use different styles of documentation. If you are unsure about which documentation style to use, ask your instructor.

- **MLA** (Modern Language Association) is the preferred style in the humanities and fine arts (see Chapter 14).
- **APA** (American Psychological Association) is followed in the social sciences and education (see Chapter 15).
- **CMS** (*Chicago Manual of Style*) offers flexibility in documentation style and the option of using footnote documentation (see Chapter 16).
- **CSE** (Council of Science Editors) covers all scientific disciplines (see Chapter 17).

The examples in this Five Steps overview guide follow MLA style documentation.

2 What kind of source am I using?

The major types of sources are:

- **Books** are mostly in print but may also be found in online and audio formats. A book source can mean either an entire book or a chapter inside a book.

Current Issue

Competition in American Life (Autumn 2007 issue)

Globalization 3.0
by Martin Walker
The West led the way in the second great wave of globalization after 1945, but it's no longer in command. A look at the emerging global order.

The Brief History of a Historical Novel
by Max Byrd
As he unravels the mysteries of Thomas Jefferson's character, one writer ponders the challenges and delights of historical fiction.

In Praise of the Values Voter
by Jon A. Shields

- **Scholarly journals** have traditionally been printed but are now increasingly available on online library databases.

- **Popular magazines and newspapers** are now distributed both in print and online.

LexisNexis® *Academic*

Search | Sources
General | News | Legal | Business | People
Easy Search™ | Power Search | General Search
Enter Search Terms | Search
Search Within | Select All | Clear All
Major U.S. and World Publications | Web Publications
Major World Publications (non-English) | Company
News Wire Services | SEC Filings
TV and Radio Broadcast Transcripts | Legal
Blogs

- **Library databases**, accessed through your library's Web site, contain books, scholarly journals, magazines, newspapers, government documents, company reports, illustrations, and sources of other information.

- **Other online sources** include wikis, discussion forums, blogs, online newspapers, online magazines, online government documents, and online audio, video, and multimedia resources.

- **Multimedia sources** include films, CDs, DVDs, television programs, cartoons, maps, advertisements, and performances.

3 When do I cite sources?

Quotations

Readers expect to find information about the original source for any words that are taken directly from a source. All words totalling four lines or fewer quoted from a source must be placed within quotation marks and the source must be cited.

How to cite a quotation

Let's say you read an article by Kermit Campbell and decided to quote in your paper the sentence that is highlighted in the paragraph below.

> If we abandon the critical perspective here because we see the values of one group as superior to the others', as the principal aim of composition pedagogy, then we really aren't preparing students to become—as many of my fair-skinned colleagues like to say—citizens, active participants in the shaping of our democracy. Being citizens of a democracy, in my view, shouldn't be about class, about aspiring to or being middle class; it should be about learning to live peaceably and justly with other citizens, especially with those who differ from the middle-class ideal.
>
> —Campbell, Kermit E. "There Goes the Neighborhood: Hip Hop Creepin' on a Come Up at the U." *College Composition and Communication* 58.3 (2007): 325-44. Print.

You can either mention Kermit Campbell in the text of your paper or you can place the author's name inside parentheses following the quotation. In both cases, include inside the parentheses the page number where you found the quotation.

A. Kermit Campbell argues that literacy education has a broader purpose than economic empowerment: "Being citizens of a democracy, in my view, shouldn't be about class, about aspiring to or being middle class; it should be about learning to live peaceably and justly with other citizens" (339).

B. An influential scholar concludes, "Being citizens of a democracy, in my view, shouldn't be about class, about aspiring to or being middle class; it should be about learning to live peaceably and justly with other citizens" (Campbell 339).

Quotations longer than four lines in MLA style are indented one inch instead of being placed within quotation marks. See page 71.

Ideas that you summarize or paraphrase

When you use information or ideas from a source, cite that source even if you do not use the writer's exact words. Any of the writer's key words or phrases that you do use should be in quotation marks.

How to cite a summary or paraphrase

Note the specific page where the idea appears.

The underlying causes of identity theft lie in the systems we use for storing data (Solove 115).

Facts that are not common knowledge or are unfamiliar to your readers

The source of facts that aren't generally known or are unfamiliar to your readers should be cited. That the Battle of Gettysburg was fought from June 30 to July 3, 1863, is common knowledge, but that some of Robert E. Lee's generals urged that the battle be fought elsewhere is likely to be unfamiliar to those who haven't studied Civil War history; thus the source needs to be cited.

How to cite the source of a fact

Note the specific page where the fact appears.

> Shakespeare may have drawn the plot of *King Lear* from a widely discussed lawsuit in 1603, when the elder daughters of feeble Brian Annesley attempted to take over his estate and were opposed by Annesley's youngest daughter, Cordell (Greenblatt 357).

4 How do I cite a source in my paper?

Citing sources is a two-part process. When readers find a reference to a source in the body of your paper, they can turn to the list of sources at the end and find the full publication information. This list is called "Works Cited" in MLA and "References" in APA.

This example quotes a passage from page 196 of the book *Emergence: The Connected Lives of Ants, Brains, Cities, and Software*, by Steven Johnson.

In-text citation

> Describing humans as "innate mind readers," one observer argues that "our skill at imagining other people's mental states ranks up there with our knack for language and our opposable thumbs" (Johnson 196).

Entry in the works-cited list

> Works Cited
>
> Johnson, Steven. *Emergence: The Connected Lives of Ants, Brains, Cities, and Software*. New York: Scribner's, 2001. Print.

How to cite an entire work, a Web site, or other electronic source

If you wish to cite an entire work (a book, a film, a performance, and so on), a Web site, or an electronic source that has no page numbers or paragraph numbers, MLA prefers that you mention the name of a person (for example, the author or director) in your paper with a corresponding entry in the works-cited list. You do not need to include the author's name in parentheses. If you cannot identify the author, mention the title in your paper.

Author's name mentioned in your paper

Michelle Tsai observes that while nonalphabetic languages cannot have spelling bees, Chinese children participate in dictionary contests and Japanese children compete in various writing and pronunciation skills.

Works Cited

Tsai, Michelle. "Bees Overseas." *Slate*. Washington Post Newsweek Interactive, 29 May 2007. Web. 7 Mar. 2009.

5 How do I cite sources at the end of my paper?

During your research you will need to collect information about each source to create your works-cited list. Go through your paper and find every reference to a work external to your paper. Each reference should have an entry in your works-cited list.

Organize your works-cited list alphabetically by authors' last names or, if no author is listed, the first word in the title other than *a, an*, or *the*. (See pages 103–104 for a sample works-cited list.) MLA style uses four basic forms for entries in the works-cited list: books, periodicals (scholarly journals, newspapers, magazines), online library database sources, and other online sources (wikis, discussion forums, blogs, online newspapers, online magazines, online government documents, and online audio, video, and multimedia resources).

Works-Cited Entries for Books

Entries for books have three main elements.

Sterling, Bruce. *Shaping Things*. Cambridge: MIT P, 2005. Print.

1. Author's name.

- List the author's name with the last name first, followed by a period.

2. Title of book.

- Find the exact title on the title page, not on the cover.
- Separate the title and subtitle with a colon.
- Italicize the title and put a period at the end.

3. Publication information.

- The place (usually the city) of publication,
- The name of the publisher,
- The date of publication.
  Use a colon after the place of publication; the publisher's name (using accepted abbreviations) is followed by a comma and the date.
- The medium of publication (*Print*).

Works-Cited Entries for Periodicals

Entries for periodicals (scholarly journals, newspapers, magazines) have three main elements.

Swearingen, C. Jan. "Feminisms and Composition." *College Composition and Communication* 57.3 (2006): 543-51. Print.

1. Author's name.

- List the author's name with the last name first, followed by a period.

2. "Title of article."

- Place the title of the article inside quotation marks.
- Insert a period before the closing quotation mark.

3. Publication information.

- Italicize the title of the journal.
- For scholarly journals follow immediately with the volume and issue numbers, and the date of publication, in parentheses, followed by a colon.
- List the page numbers, followed by a period. Use a hyphen in the page range.
- List the medium of publication (*Print*).

Works-Cited Entries for Library Database Sources

Basic entries for library database sources have four main elements.

Stein, Rob. "Social Networks' Sway May Be Underestimated." *Washington Post* 26 May 2008, suburban ed.: A6. *LexisNexis Academic*. Web. 3 Apr. 2009.

1. Author's name.

- List the author's name with the last name first, followed by a period.

2. "Title of article."

- Place the title of the article inside quotation marks.
- Insert a period before the closing quotation mark.

3. Print publication information.

- Give the print publication information in standard format, in this case for a newspaper (see page 84).

4. Database information.

- Italicize the name of the database, followed by a period.
- For all database sources, the medium of publication is *Web*.
- List the date you accessed the source (day, month, and year).

Works-Cited Entries for Other Online Sources

Basic entries for online sources (wikis, discussion forums, blogs, online publications, online government documents, and online audio, video, and multimedia resources) have three main elements. Sometimes information such as the author's name or the date of publication is missing from the online source. Include the information you are able to locate.

There are many formats for the various kinds of electronic publications. Here is the format of an entry for an article on the Web.

> Smith, Patrick. "Ask the Pilot." *Salon.com*. Salon, 1 June 2007.
> Web. 6 Apr. 2009.

1. Author's name.

- List the author's name with the last name first, followed by a period.

2. "Title of work"; *Title of the overall Web site.*

- Place the title of work inside quotation marks if it is part of a larger Web site.
- Italicize the name of the overall site if it is different from the title of work.
- Some Web sites are updated, so list the version if you find it (e.g., *2009* ed.).

3. Publication information.

- List the publisher or sponsor of the site followed by a comma. If not available, use *N.p.* (for *no publisher*).
- List the date of publication if available; if not, use *n.d.*
- List the medium of publication (*Web*).
- List the date you accessed the source (day, month, and year).

APA style includes the same information in its list of references but uses a different format and includes the URL. For the format of entries in APA's list of references, see pages 110–121.

14 MLA Documentation

MLA is the preferred style in the humanities and fine arts.

14a In-text Citations in MLA Style 69

14b Books in MLA-Style Works Cited 74

14c Journals, Magazines, Newspapers, and Documents 80

JOURNALS AND MAGAZINES

The 2009 update to MLA style includes the following major changes:

- Addition of the medium of publication (*print, Web, film, photograph*, and so on) to every entry in the list of works cited.
- Use of italics instead of underlining for all titles.
- Inclusion of volume and issue numbers for every journal citation.
- Simplification of Web and database entries with no URL listed except when essential to locating the item.

If you have questions that the examples in this chapter do not address, consult the *MLA Handbook for Writers of Research Papers*, seventh edition (2009), and the *MLA Style Manual and Guide to Scholarly Publishing*, third edition (2008).

14a In-text Citations in MLA Style

Paraphrase, summary, or short quotation

A short quotation takes four lines or fewer in your paper.

> The computing power of networked technology is growing at an accelerating rate, prompting some visionaries to argue that the Internet "may actually become self-aware sometime in the next century" (Johnson 114).

Here the author's name is provided in the parenthetical reference.

> Science writer and cultural critic Steven Johnson poses the question this way: "Is the Web itself becoming a giant brain?" (114).

Note that the period goes *after* the parentheses.

The author of the quotation is named in this sentence, so only a page number is needed in the citation.

Sample in-text citations

1. Author named in your text

Put the author's name in a signal phrase in your sentence.

> Sociologist Daniel Bell called this emerging U.S. economy the "postindustrial society" (3).

2. Author not named in your text

> In 1997, the Gallup poll reported that 55% of adults in the United States think secondhand smoke is "very harmful," compared to only 36% in 1994 (Saad 4).

3. Work by one author

The author's last name comes first, followed by the page number. There is no comma.

> (Bell 3)

4. Work by two or three authors

The authors' last names follow the order of the title page. If there are two authors, join the names with *and*. If there are three, use a comma between the first two names and a comma with *and* before the last name.

> (Francisco, Vaughn, and Lynn 7)

5. Work by four or more authors

You may use the phrase *et al.* (meaning "and others") for all names but the first, or you may write out all the names.

> (Abrams et al. 1653)

6. Work by no named author

Use a shortened version of the title that includes at least the first important word so your reader can find the full title in the list of works cited.

> A review in the *New Yorker* of Ryan Adams's new album focuses on the artist's age ("Pure" 25).

"Pure" is in quotation marks because it is the shortened title of an article.

7. Work by a group or organization

Treat the group or organization as the author. Try to identify the group author in the text and place only the page number in parentheses.

> According to the *Irish Free State Handbook*, published by the Ministry for Industry and Finance, the population of Ireland in 1929 was approximately 4,192,000 (23).

8. Quotations longer than four lines

Begin quotations longer than four lines on a new line and indent one inch or ten spaces. Do not add quotation marks. Note that the period goes before the page number at the end.

> In her article "Art for Everybody," Susan Orlean attempts to explain the popularity of painter Thomas Kinkade:
>
> > People like to own things they think are valuable. . . . The high price of limited editions is part of their appeal: it implies that they are choice and exclusive, and that only a certain class of people will be able to afford them—a limited edition of people with taste and discernment. (128)
>
> This same statement could also explain the popularity of phenomena like PBS's *Antiques Road Show*.

9. Two or more works by the same author

Use the author's last name and then a shortened version of the title of each source.

> The majority of books written about coauthorship focus on partners of the same sex (Laird, *Women* 351).

Note that *Women* is italicized because it is the title of a book.

10. Different authors with the same last name

Include the initial of the first name in the parenthetical reference.

> Web surfing requires more mental involvement than channel surfing (S. Johnson 107).

11. Two or more sources within the same sentence

Place each citation directly after the statement it supports.

> Many sweeping pronouncements were made in the 1990s that the Internet is the best opportunity to improve education since the printing press (Ellsworth xxii) or even in the history of the world (Dyrli and Kinnaman 79).

12. Two or more sources within the same citation

If two sources support a single point, separate them with a semicolon.

> (McKibbin 39; Gore 92)

13. Work quoted in another source

> National governments have become increasingly what Ulrich Beck, in a 1999 interview, calls "zombie institutions"—institutions which are "dead and still alive" (qtd. in Bauman 6).

14. Web sources including Web pages, blogs, podcasts, wikis, videos, and other multimedia sources

MLA prefers that you mention the author in your text instead of putting the author's name in parentheses.

> Andrew Keen ironically used his own blog to claim that "blogs are boring to write (yawn), boring to read (yawn) and boring to discuss (yawn)."

15. Work in an anthology

Cite the name of the author of the work within an anthology, not the name of the editor of the collection.

> In "Beard," Melissa Jane Hardie explores the role assumed by Elizabeth Taylor as the celebrity companion of gay actors including Rock Hudson and Montgomery Clift (278-79).

16. Classic works

To supply a reference to classic works, you sometimes need more than a page number from a specific edition. (Readers should be able to locate a quotation in any edition of the book.) Give the page number from the edition that you are using, then other identifying information.

> "Marriage is a house" is one of the most memorable lines in *Don Quixote* (546; pt. 2, bk. 3, ch. 19).

14b Books in MLA-Style Works Cited

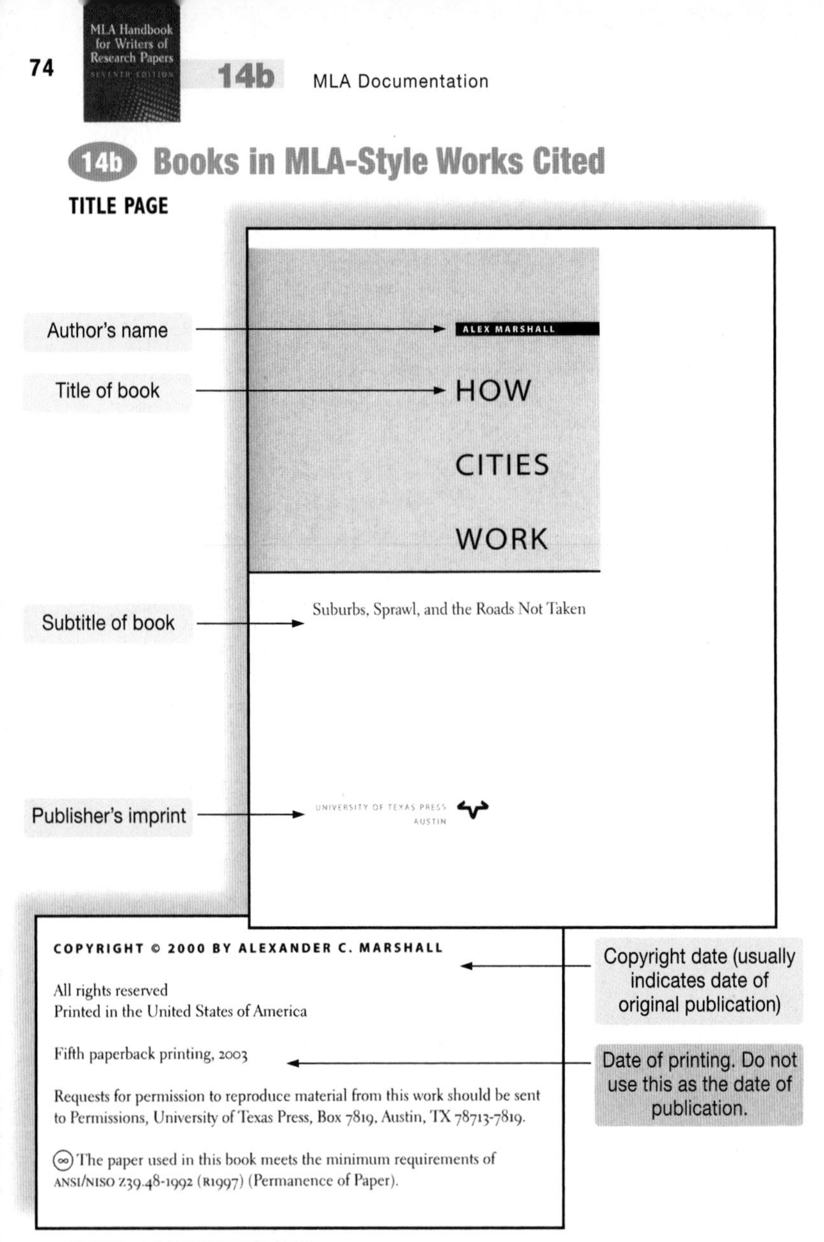

Marshall, Alex. *How Cities Work: Suburbs, Sprawl, and the Roads Not Taken*. Austin: U of Texas P, 2000. Print.

AUTHOR'S OR EDITOR'S NAME

The author's last name comes first, followed by a comma and the first name.

For edited books, put the abbreviation *ed.* after the name, preceded by a comma:

Kavanagh, **Peter**, **ed**.

BOOK TITLE

Use the exact title, as it appears on the title page (not the cover).

Underline the title.

All nouns, verbs, pronouns, adjectives, adverbs, and subordinating conjunctions, and the first word of the title are capitalized. Do not capitalize articles, prepositions, or coordinating conjunctions unless they are the first word of the title or subtitle.

PUBLICATION INFORMATION

Place of publication

If more than one city is given, use the first.

For cities outside the U.S., add an abbreviation of the country or province if the city is not well known.

Publisher

Use a short form of the name. For example, shorten *Addison, Wesley, Longman* to *Longman; W. W. Norton & Co.* to *Norton*.

Omit words such as *Publisher* and *Inc*.

For university presses, use *UP*: **New York UP**

Date of publication

Give the year as it appears on the copyright page. If no year is given, put *n.d.* ("no date"): **Cambridge: Harvard UP, n.d.**

Medium of publication

Print.

Sample works-cited entries for books

17. Book by one author

Friedman, Alice T. *Women and the Making of the Modern House*. New Haven: Yale UP, 2007. Print.

18. Two or more books by the same author

In the entry for the first book, include the author's name. In the second entry, substitute three hyphens and a period for the author's name. List the titles of books by the same author in alphabetical order.

Grimsley, Jim. *Boulevard*. Chapel Hill: Algonquin, 2002. Print.

---. *Dream Boy*. New York: Simon, 1995. Print.

19. Book by two or three authors

The second and subsequent authors' names appear first name first.

Burger, Edward B., and Michael Starbird. *Coincidences, Chaos, and All That Math Jazz*. New York: Norton, 2006. Print.

20. Book by four or more authors

You may use the phrase *et al.* (meaning "and others") for all authors but the first, or you may write out all the names. Use the same method in the in-text citation as you do in the works-cited list.

North, Stephen M., et al. *Refiguring the Ph.D. in English Studies*. Urbana: NCTE, 2000. Print.

21. Book by an unknown author

Begin the entry with the title.

Encyclopedia of Americana. New York: Somerset, 2001. Print.

22. Book by a group or organization

Treat the group as the author of the work.

United Nations. *The Charter of the United Nations: A Commentary*. New York: Oxford UP, 2000. Print.

23. Title within a title

If the title contains the title of another book or a word normally italicized, do not underline that title or word.

Higgins, Brian, and Hershel Parker. *Critical Essays on Herman Melville's* Moby-Dick. New York: Hall, 1992. Print.

24. Book with no publication date

If no year of publication is given but it can be approximated, put *c.* ("circa") and the approximate date in brackets: [c. 1999]. Otherwise, put *n.d.* ("no date").

O'Sullivan, Colin. *Traditions and Novelties of the Irish Country Folk*. Dublin, [c. 1793]. Print.

James, Franklin. *In the Valley of the King*. Cambridge: Harvard UP, n.d. Print.

25. Reprinted works

For works of fiction that have been printed in many different editions or reprints, give the original publication date after the title.

Wilde, Oscar. *The Picture of Dorian Gray*. 1890. New York: Norton, 2001. Print.

26. Introduction, foreword, preface, or afterword

Give the author and then the name of the specific part being cited. Next, name the book. Then, if the author for the whole work is different, put that author's name after the word *By*. Place inclusive page numbers at the end.

Benstock, Sheri. Introduction. *The House of Mirth*. By Edith Wharton. Boston: Bedford-St. Martin's, 2002. 3-24. Print.

27. Selection from an anthology or edited collection

Sedaris, David. "Full House." *The Best American Nonrequired Reading 2004*. Ed. Dave Eggers. Boston: Houghton, 2004. 350-58. Print.

28. More than one selection from an anthology or edited collection

Multiple selections from a single anthology can be handled by creating a complete entry for the anthology and shortened cross-references for individual works in that anthology.

Adichie, Chimamanda Ngozi. "Half of a Yellow Sun." Eggers 1-17.

Eggers, Dave, ed. *The Best American Nonrequired Reading 2004*. Boston: Houghton, 2004. Print.

Sedaris, David. "Full House." Eggers 350-58.

29. Article in a reference work

You can omit the names of editors and most publishing information for an article from a familiar reference work. Identify the edition by date. There is no need to give the page numbers when a work is arranged alphabetically. Give the author's name, if known.

"Utilitarianism." *The Columbia Encyclopedia*. 6th ed. 2001. Print.

30. Religious texts

Italicize the Bible and other titles of sacred texts only when you are citing a specific edition.

The New Oxford Annotated Bible. Ed. Bruce M. Metzger and Roland E. Murphy. New York: Oxford UP, 1991. Print.

31. Book with an editor

List an edited book under the editor's name if your focus is on the editor. Otherwise, cite an edited book under the author's name as shown in the second example.

Lewis, Gifford, ed. *The Big House of Inver.* By Edith Somerville and Martin Ross. Dublin: Farmar, 2000. Print.

Somerville, Edith, and Martin Ross. *The Big House of Inver.* Ed. Gifford Lewis. Dublin: Farmar, 2000. Print.

32. Book with a translator

Mallarmé, Stéphane. *Divagations.* Trans. Barbara Johnson. Cambridge: Harvard UP, 2007. Print.

33. Second or subsequent edition of a book

Hawthorn, Jeremy, ed. *A Concise Glossary of Contemporary Literary Theory.* 3rd ed. London: Arnold, 2001. Print.

34. Multivolume work

Samuel, Raphael. *Theatres of Memory.* Vol. 1. London: Verso, 1999. Print.

35. Illustrated book or graphic narrative

After the title of the book, give the illustrator's name, preceded by the abbreviation *Illus.* If the emphasis is on the illustrator's work, place the illustrator's name first, followed by the abbreviation *illus.*, and list the author after the title, preceded by the word *By.*

Strunk, William, Jr., and E. B. White. *The Elements of Style Illustrated.* Illus. Maira Kalman. New York: Penguin, 2005. Print.

14c Journals, Magazines, Newspapers, and Documents in MLA-Style Works Cited

JOURNAL COVER

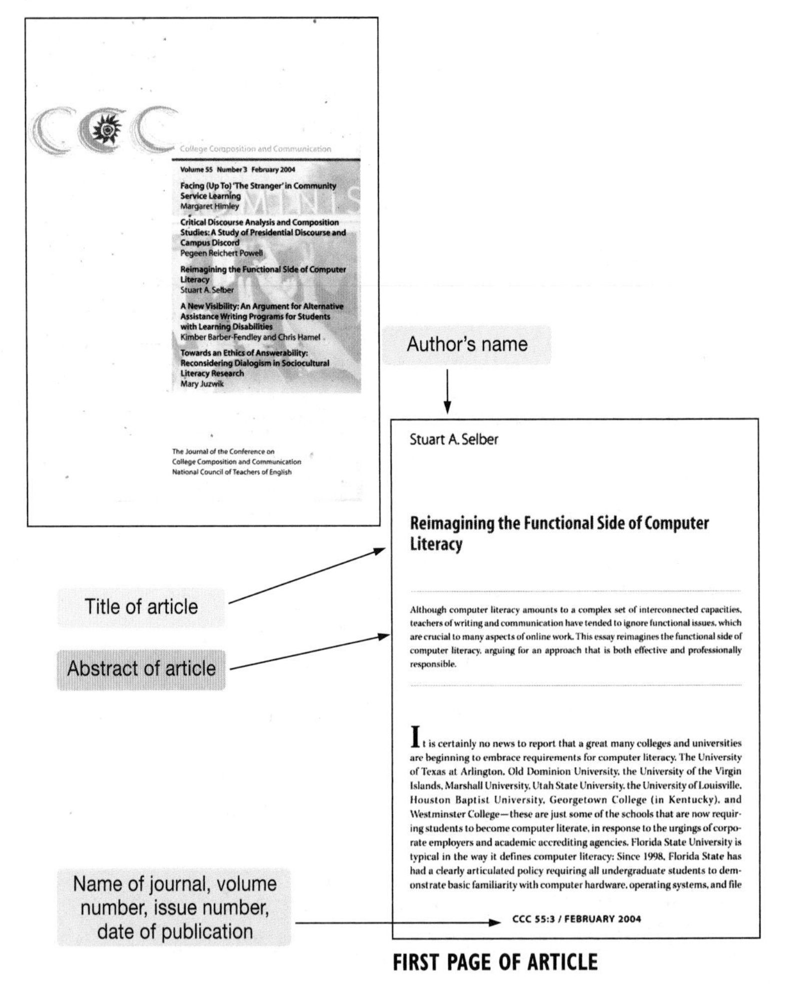

Stuart A. Selber

Reimagining the Functional Side of Computer Literacy

Although computer literacy amounts to a complex set of interconnected capacities, teachers of writing and communication have tended to ignore functional issues, which are crucial to many aspects of online work. This essay reimagines the functional side of computer literacy, arguing for an approach that is both effective and professionally responsible.

It is certainly no news to report that a great many colleges and universities are beginning to embrace requirements for computer literacy. The University of Texas at Arlington, Old Dominion University, the University of the Virgin Islands, Marshall University, Utah State University, the University of Louisville, Houston Baptist University, Georgetown College (in Kentucky), and Westminster College—these are just some of the schools that are now requiring students to become computer literate, in response to the urgings of corporate employers and academic accrediting agencies. Florida State University is typical in the way it defines computer literacy: Since 1998, Florida State has had a clearly articulated policy requiring all undergraduate students to demonstrate basic familiarity with computer hardware, operating systems, and file

CCC 55:3 / FEBRUARY 2004

FIRST PAGE OF ARTICLE

Selber, Stuart A. "Reimagining the Functional Side of Computer Literacy." *CCC* 55.3 (2004): 470-503. Print.

AUTHOR'S NAME

The author's last name comes first, followed by a comma and the first name.

For two or more works by the same author, consult the sample works-cited list on page 103.

TITLE OF ARTICLE

Use the exact title, which appears at the top of the article.

Put the title in quotation marks. If a book title is part of the article's title, underline the book title. If a title requiring quotation marks is part of the article's title, use single quotation marks.

All nouns, verbs, pronouns, adjectives, adverbs, and subordinating conjunctions, and the first word of the title and any subtitle are capitalized. Do not capitalize articles, prepositions, or coordinating conjunctions unless they are the first word of the title.

PUBLICATION INFORMATION

Name of journal

Italicize the title of the journal.

Abbreviate the title of the journal if it commonly appears that way (as in this example).

Volume, issue, and page numbers

- For scholarly journals give the volume number and issue number. Place a period between the volume and issue numbers: "55.3" indicates volume 55, issue 3.
- Some scholarly journals use issue numbers only.
- Give the page numbers for the entire article, not just the part you used.

Date of publication

- For magazines and journals identified by the month or season of publication, use the month (or season) and year in place of the volume.
- For weekly or biweekly magazines, give both the day and month of publication, as listed on the issue. Note that the day precedes the month and no comma is used.

Medium of publication

Print.

Sample works-cited entries for journals and magazines

36. Article by one author

Bhabha, Jacqueline. "The Child—What Sort of Human?" *PMLA* 121.5 (2006): 1526-35. Print.

37. Article by two or three authors

Shamoo, Adil E., and Jonathan D. Moreo. "Ethics of Research Involving Mandatory Drug Testing of High School Athletes in Oregon." *American Journal of Bioethics* 4.1 (2004): 25-31. Print.

38. Article by four or more authors

You may use the phrase *et al.* (meaning "and others") for all authors but the first, or you may write out all the names.

Breece, Katherine E., et al. "Patterns of mtDNA Diversity in Northwestern North America." *Human Biology* 76.5 (2004): 33-54. Print.

39. Article by an unknown author

"Idol Gossip." *People* 12 Apr. 2004: 34-35. Print.

40. Monthly or seasonal magazines or journals

Use the month (or season) and year in place of the volume. Abbreviate the names of all months except May, June, and July.

Barlow, John Perry. "Africa Rising: Everything You Know about Africa Is Wrong." *Wired* Jan. 1998: 142-58. Print.

41. Weekly or biweekly magazines

For weekly or biweekly magazines, give both the day and month of publication, as listed on the issue.

Toobin, Jeffrey. "Crackdown." *New Yorker* 5 Nov. 2001: 56-61. Print.

42. Article in a scholarly journal

List the volume and issue numbers after the name of the journal.

Duncan, Mike. "Whatever Happened to the Paragraph?" *College English* 69.5 (2007): 470-95. Print.

43. Article in a scholarly journal that uses only issue numbers

List the issue number after the name of the journal.

McCall, Sophie. "Double Vision Reading." *Canadian Literature* 194 (2007): 95-97. Print.

44. Review

If there is no title, just name the work reviewed.

Mendelsohn, Daniel. "The Two Oscar Wildes." Rev. of *The Importance of Being Earnest*, dir. Oliver Parker. *New York Review of Books* 10 Oct. 2002: 23-24. Print.

45. Letter to the editor

Patai, Daphne. Letter. *Harper's Magazine* Dec. 2001: 4. Print.

46. Editorial

"Stop Stonewalling on Reform." Editorial. *Business Week* 17 June 2002: 108. Print.

Sample works-cited entries for newspapers

47. Article by one author

Boyd, Robert S. "Solar System Has a Double." *Montreal Gazette* 14 June 2002, final ed.: A1. Print.

48. Article by two or three authors

Davis, Howard, June Allstead, and Jane Mavis. "Rice's Testimony to 9/11 Commission Leaves Unanswered Questions." *Dallas Morning News* 9 Apr. 2004, final ed.: C5. Print.

49. Article by an unknown author

"Democratic Candidates Debate Iraq War." *Austin American-Statesman* 19 Jan. 2004: A6. Print.

50. Article that continues to a nonconsecutive page

Add a plus sign after the number of the first page.

Kaplow, Larry, and Tasgola Karla Bruner. "U.S.: Don't Let Taliban Forces Flee." *Austin American-Statesman* 20 Nov. 2001, final ed.: A11+. Print.

51. Review

Fox, Nichols. "What's for Dinner?" Rev. of *Eating in the Dark: America's Experiment with Genetically Engineered Food*, by Kathleen Hart. *Washington Post* 16 June 2002, final ed.: T9. Print.

52. Letter to the editor

Leach, Richard E. Letter. *Boston Globe* 2 Apr. 2007, first ed.: A10. Print.

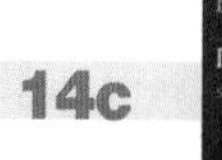

53. Editorial

"Dream On?" Editorial. *Washington Post* 27 July 2008, final ed.: B6. Print.

Sample works-cited entries for documents

54. Government document

United States. General Services Administration. *Consumer Action Handbook*. Washington: GPO, 2008. Print.

55. *Congressional Record*

Cong. Rec. 8 Feb. 2000: 1222-46. Print.

56. Bulletin or pamphlet

The Common Cold. Austin: U of Texas Health Center, 2007. Print.

57. Published letter

Wilde, Oscar. "To Lord Alfred Douglas." 17 Feb. 1895. In *The Complete Letters of Oscar Wilde*. Ed. Merlin Holland and Rupert Hart-Davis. New York: Holt, 2000. 632-33. Print.

58. Published dissertation or thesis

Mason, Jennifer. *Civilized Creatures: Animality, Cultural Power, and American Literature, 1850-1901*. Diss. U of Texas at Austin, 2000. Ann Arbor: UMI, 2000. Print.

14d Library Database Sources in MLA-Style Works Cited

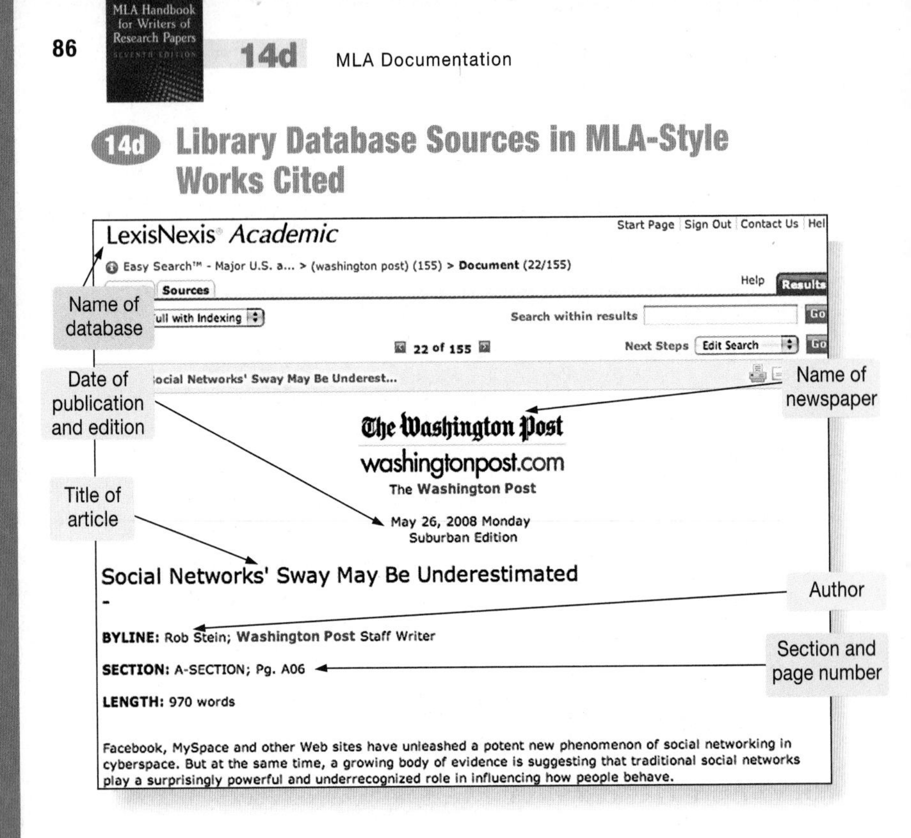

59. Journal article from a library database

Snider, Michael. "Wired to Another World." *Maclean's* 3 Mar. 2003: 23-24. *Academic Search Premier*. Web. 9 Feb. 2009.

60. Newspaper article from a library database

Sahagun, Louis. "A High-Water Mark for Mono Lake." *Los Angeles Times* 28 July 2008: B1. *ProQuest Newspapers*. Web. 23 Jan. 2009.

Stein, Rob. "Social Networks' Sway May Be Underestimated." *Washington Post* 26 May 2008, suburban ed.: A6. *LexisNexis Academic.* Web. 30 Mar. 2009.

AUTHOR'S NAME

The author's last name comes first, followed by a comma and the first name.

For two or more works by the same author, consult the sample works-cited list on page 103.

TITLE OF ARTICLE

Use the exact title, which appears at the top of the article.

Put the title in quotation marks. If a book title is part of the article's title, italicize the book title. If a title requiring quotation marks is part of the article's title, use single quotation marks.

PUBLICATION INFORMATION

Name of journal or newspaper

Italicize the title of the journal or newspaper.

Abbreviate the title of the journal or newspaper if it commonly appears that way.

Volume, issue, date, and page numbers

List the same information you would for a print item.

DATABASE INFORMATION

Name of database

Italicize the name of the database, followed by a period.

Medium of publication

For all database sources, the medium of publication is *Web*.

Date of access

List the date you accessed the source (day, month, and year).

14e Web Publications in MLA-Style Works Cited

HOME PAGE

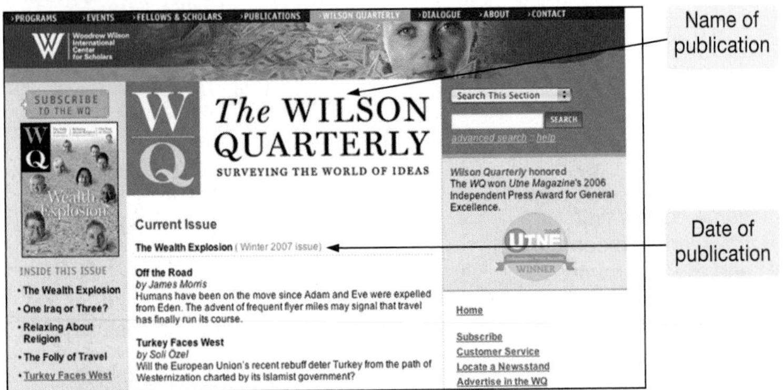

FIRST PAGE OF THE ARTICLE

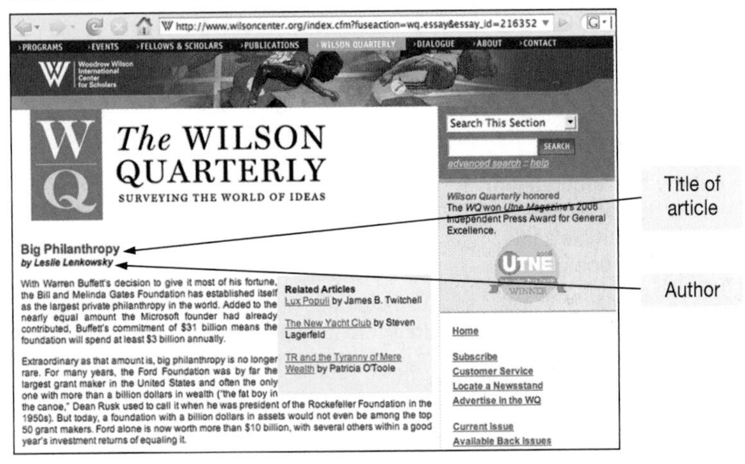

Lenkowsky, Leslie. "Big Philanthropy." *Wilson Quarterly*. Woodrow Wilson Center, Winter 2007. Web. 7 Jan. 2009.

AUTHOR'S NAME

Authorship is sometimes hard to discern for online sources. If you know the author or creator, follow the rules for books and journals.

If the only authority you find is a group or organization, list its name after the date of publication or last revision.

TITLE OF THE WORK AND TITLE OF THE OVERALL WEB SITE

Place the title of the work inside quotation marks if it is part of a larger Web site.

Untitled works may be identified by a label (e.g., *Home page, Introduction*). List the label in the title slot without quotation marks or italics.

Italicize the name of the overall site if it is different from the work. The name of the overall Web site will usually be found on its index or home page.

Some Web sites are updated, so list the version if you find it (e.g., *Vers. 1.2*).

PUBLICATION INFORMATION

List the publisher's or sponsor's name followed by a comma. If it isn't available, use *N.p.*

List the date of publication by day, month, and year if available. If you cannot find a date, use *n.d.*

Give the medium of publication (*Web*).

List the date you accessed the site by day, month, and year.

When do you list a URL?

MLA style no longer requires including URLs of Web sources in reference citations. URLs are of limited value because they change frequently and they can be specific to an individual search. Include the URL as supplementary information only when your readers probably cannot locate the source without the URL.

Sample works-cited entries for online publications

61. Publication by a known author

Boerner, Steve. "Leopold Mozart." *The Mozart Project: Biography*. Mozart Project, 21 Mar. 1998. Web. 30 Oct. 2008.

62. Publication by a group or organization

If a work has no author's or editor's name listed, begin the entry with the title.

"State of the Birds." *Audubon*. National Audubon Society, 2008. Web. 19 Aug. 2008.

63. Publication on the Web with print publication data

Include the print publication information. Then give the name of the Web site or database in italics, the medium of publication (*Web*), and the date of access (day, month, and year).

Kirsch, Irwin S., et al. *Adult Literacy in America*. Darby: Diane, 1993. *Google Scholar*. Web. 30 Oct. 2008.

64. Article in a scholarly journal on the Web

Some scholarly journals are published on the Web only. List articles by author, title, name of journal in italics, volume and issue number, and year of publication. If the journal does not have page numbers, use *n. pag.* in place of page numbers. Then list the medium of publication (*Web*) and the date of access (day, month, and year).

> Fleckenstein, Kristie. "Who's Writing? Aristotelian Ethos and the Author Position in Digital Poetics." *Kairos* 11.3 (2007): n. pag. Web. 6 Apr. 2008.

65. Article in a newspaper on the Web

List the name of the newspaper in italics, followed by a period and the publisher's name. Follow the publisher's name with a comma. If no publisher is available, use *N.p.* The first date is the date of publication; the second is the date of access.

> Brown, Patricia Leigh. "Australia in Sonoma." *New York Times.* New York Times, 5 July 2008. Web. 3 Aug. 2009.

66. Article in a magazine on the Web

> Brown, Patricia Leigh. "The Wild Horse Is Us." *Newsweek.* Newsweek, 1 July 2008. Web. 12 Dec. 2008.

67. Book on the Web

If the book was printed and then scanned, give the print publication information. Then give the name of the database or Web site in italics, the medium of publication (*Web*), and the date of access (day, month, and year).

> Prebish, Charles S., and Kenneth K. Tanaka. *The Faces of Buddhism in America*. Berkeley: U of California P, 2003. *eScholarship Editions*. Web. 2 May 2009.

68. Document within a scholarly project or archive

Give the print information, then the title of the scholarly project or archive in italics, the medium of publication (*Web*), and the date of access (day, month, and year).

> "New York Quiet." *Franklin Repository* 5 Aug. 1863, 1. *Valley of the Shadow*. Web. 23 Feb. 2009.

69. PDFs and digital files

PDFs and other digital files often can be downloaded through links. Determine the kind of work you are citing, include the appropriate information for the particular kind of work, and list the type of file.

> Glaser, Edward L., and Albert Saiz. "The Rise of the Skilled City." Discussion Paper No. 2025. Harvard Institute of Economic Research. Cambridge: Harvard U, 2003. PDF file.

70. Government publication on the Web

If you cannot locate the author of the document, give the name of the government and agency that published it.

> United States. Dept. of Health and Human Services. *Salmonellosis Outbreak in Certain Types of Tomatoes*. US Dept. of Health and Human Services, 5 July 2008. Web. 30 Nov. 2008.

14f Unedited Online Sources in MLA-Style Works Cited

71. Wiki entry

Wiki content is written collaboratively, thus no author is listed. Because the content on Wiki changes frequently, Wikis are not considered reliable scholarly sources.

"Snowboard." *Wikipedia*. Wikimedia Foundation, 2009. Web. 30 Jan. 2009.

72. Online synchronous communication (MUDs, MOOs)

Give the name of the author (even if it is a pseudonym), the title, the name of the forum in italics, the publisher if available, the date of the posting, the medium, and the date of access.

Sirius, B. "Discussion of the Popularity of *Harry Potter*." *LinguaMOO*. U of Texas at Dallas, 12 Dec. 2000. Web. 24 Nov. 2004.

73. E-mail

Give the name of the writer, the subject line, a description of the message, the date, and the medium of delivery (*E-mail*).

Ballmer, Steve. "A New Era of Business Productivity and Innovation." Message to Microsoft Executive E-mail. 30 Nov. 2006. E-mail.

74. Posting to a discussion list

Give the name of the writer, the subject line, the name of the list in italics, the publisher, the date of the posting, the medium (*Web*), and the date of access.

Dobrin, Sid. "Re: ecocomposition?" *Writing Program Administration*. Arizona State U, 19 Dec. 2008. Web. 5 Jan. 2009.

75. Course home page

Sparks, Julie. "English Composition 1B." Course home page. San Jose State U, Fall 2008. Web. 17 Sept. 2008.

76. Personal home page

List *Home page* without quotation marks in place of the title. If no date is listed, use *n.d.*

Graff, Harvey J. Home page. Dept. of English, Ohio State U, n.d. Web. 15 Nov. 2008.

77. Blog entry

If there is no sponsor or publisher for the blog, use *N.p.*

Arrington, Michael. "Think Before You Voicemail." *TechCrunch*. N.p., 5 July 2008. Web. 10 Sept. 2008.

14g Visual and Multimedia Sources in MLA-Style Works Cited

78. Cartoon or comic strip

Give the author's name, the title of the cartoon or comic strip in quotation marks, and the description *Cartoon* or *Comic strip*.

Trudeau, G. B. "Doonesbury." Comic strip. *Washington Post* 21 Apr. 2008. C15. Print.

79. Advertisement

Begin with the name of the advertiser or product, then the word *Advertisement.*

Nike. Advertisement. ABC. 8 Oct. 2008. Television.

80. Map, graph, or chart

List *Map, Graph,* or *Chart* after the title.

Greenland. Map. Vancouver: International Travel Maps, 2004. Print.

81. Map on the Web

"Lansing, Michigan." Map. *Google Maps.* Google, 2008. Web.
3 Nov. 2008.

82. Painting, sculpture, or photograph

Give the artist's name first, the title of the work in italics, the year of its creation, the medium of composition, the name of the institution that houses the work and the city, or the name of the collection.

Manet, Edouard. *Olympia.* 1863. Oil on canvas. Musée d'Orsay, Paris.

83. Sound recording

McCoury, Del, perf. "1952 Vincent Black Lightning." By Richard Thompson.
Del and the Boys. Ceili, 2001. CD.

84. Podcast

Sussingham, Robin. "All Things Autumn." No. 2. *HighLifeUtah.* N.p.,
20 Nov. 2006. Web. 28 Feb. 2009.

85. Video on the Web

Video on the Web often lacks a creator and a date. Begin the entry with a title if you cannot find a creator. Use *n.d.* if you cannot find a date.

Wesch, Michael. *A Vision of Students Today*. *YouTube*. YouTube, 2007. Web. 28 May 2008.

86. Film

Begin with the title in italics. List the director, the distributor, the date, and the medium. Other data, such as the names of the screenwriters and performers, is optional.

Wanted. Dir. Timur Bekmambetov. Perf. James McAvoy, Angelina Jolie, and Morgan Freeman. Universal, 2008. Film.

87. DVD

No Country for Old Men. Dir. Joel Coen and Ethan Coen. Perf. Tommy Lee Jones, Javier Bardem, and Josh Brolin. Paramount, 2007. DVD.

88. Television or radio program

"Kaisha." *The Sopranos*. Perf. James Gandolfini, Lorraine Bracco, and Edie Falco. HBO. 4 June 2006. Television.

89. Broadcast interview

Cage, Nicolas. Interview with Terry Gross. *Fresh Air*. WHYY-FM, Philadelphia. 13 June 2002. Radio.

90. Speech, debate, mediated discussion, or public talk

Clinton, William Jefferson. Liz Carpenter Distinguished Lecture Series, U of Texas at Austin. 12 Feb. 2003. Address.

14h Sample Research Paper with MLA Documentation

FORMATTING A RESEARCH PAPER IN MLA STYLE

MLA offers these general guidelines for formatting a research paper.

- **Use white, 8½-by-11-inch paper.** Don't use colored or lined paper.
- **Double-space everything—the title, headings, body of the paper, quotations, and works-cited list.** Set the line spacing on your word processor for double spacing and leave it there.
- **Put your last name and the page number at the top of every page, aligned with the right margin, one-half inch from the top of the page.** Your word processor has a header command that will automatically put a header with the page number on every page.
- **Specify one-inch margins.** One-inch margins are the default setting for most word processors.
- **Do not justify (make even) the right margin.** Justifying the right margin throws off the spacing between words and makes your paper harder to read. Use the left-align setting instead.
- **Indent the first line of each paragraph one-half inch (5 spaces).** Set the paragraph indent command or the tab on the ruler of your word processor at one-half inch.
- **Use the same readable typeface throughout your paper.** Use a standard typeface such as Times New Roman, 12 point.
- **Use block format for quotations longer than four lines.** See page 71.
- **MLA does not require a title page.** Unless your instructor asks for a separate title page, put one inch from the top of the page your name, your instructor's name, the course, and the date on separate lines. Center your title on the next line. Do not underline your title or put it inside quotation marks.

MLA style does not require a title page. Check with your instructor to find out whether you need one.

Include your last name and page number as page header, beginning with the first page, 1/2″ from the top.

Cruz 1

Cecilia Cruz

Professor Semler

English 1302

5 May 2009

Privacy in Public

Center the title. Do not underline the title, put it inside quotation marks, or type it in all capital letters.

Current attitudes toward the issue of privacy often promote imbalances of power that allow injustice to escape public view. In particular, technologies for video and data surveillance create zones of inequality where some individuals are given great power while others are subjected to that power. Even as society becomes more open, surveillance technologies enable those in power to extend to the public sphere the unequal relations that have historically been limited to the private sphere. Understanding the issues of technology and privacy is the first step toward correcting the abuses of surveillance technologies.

Cruz's thesis is stated at the end of the first paragraph.

Increased access to communication technologies has, in theory, the potential to make inequality more visible and more open to public scrutiny. This potential, however, has not been realized. Instead, more and more information has been defined as private and therefore escaping public scrutiny, leading to what Helen Jones calls the "paradox" of "systematic surveillance and abuse" (590). The paradox at the intersection

Cruz 2

of surveillance and privacy can be described this way: surveillance systems not only invade the privacy of individuals, in terms of making their personal information accessible, they also create spaces where acts of inequality can go unnoticed. Surveillance technologies like CCTV (closed-circuit television), which is used to remotely watch and sometimes record others' actions, and data-mining, which is the largely automated process of collecting information about an individual from publicly available sources, are two examples of the extension of "private" power and control into the public sphere (where "public" is any space that is open and shared by all). Video surveillance extends the unequal power relationships of private life into public areas by allowing those who run the cameras to have an inordinate amount of control over individuals they are watching. Similarly, automated data collection for the purposes of advertising and other, more nefarious ends operates largely hidden from public scrutiny.

There are three distinct features of surveillance technologies that contribute to the "privatizing" of public spaces. First, surveillance technologies create unequal power relations by making the observed subject accessible to the observer while simultaneously making the observer inaccessible. One example of this power imbalance is voyeurism by CCTV

Specify 1″ margins all around. Double-space everything.

Indent each paragraph five spaces (1/2″ on the ruler in your word processing program).

Cruz 3

Cite publications by the name of the author (or authors).

operators (Koskela 301). As Katharine Mieszkowski points out in an article on webcams, the unobtrusive gaze of the camera "can turn anyone into a sex object . . . without their ever being aware of it." By making individuals subject to the gaze of camera operators, the sexualizing potential of video surveillance has extended the inequality of private spaces into the public sphere. While this inequality existed in many forms before the widespread adoption of video surveillance technologies, these technologies greatly increase the scope and power of this intrusion.

Similarly, automated data collection has made it possible for web companies to collect detailed information about users' "preferences, hopes, worries and fears," most often doing so without those users' knowledge (Story, "Internet"). The highly publicized negative reaction to the introduction of Facebook's Beacon advertising system, in which the social networking site made users' spending habits visible to online friends, occurred only because the company's collection of user data was made public (Story, "Internet"). Marketers have recently begun to provide ways for consumers to opt out of behavioral surveillance (Story, "Online"), but this transparency is not the norm. Like CCTV surveillance, the secrecy and anonymity of online data collection creates a paradoxical situation where users' privacy is surrendered while the privacy of the observer is protected.

If more than one publication is by the same author, include an abbreviated title in the reference.

Cruz 4

Second, surveillance technologies create a "private" space for the observer that is largely unregulated and free from public scrutiny. One observer of video surveillance notes that police officials are able to avoid checks to their power by commandeering private surveillance tapes. In other words, "what would be lawful taping by individuals would not be lawful by the government," but government officials "can get access to private videotapes" for policing purposes (Lee). In this area that exists outside of warrant and wiretapping laws, government officials can commandeer private data that they would not have been legally able to collect and use against individuals in investigations.

Do not include page numbers for items on a single page or without pagination such as a Web site.?

Third, the possibility of voyeuristic surveillance transforms public spaces into areas of domination and control. One resident of the United Kingdom who complained about the rampant use of CCTV in that country claimed that when citizens do not know who is observing them, they will "censure [*sic*] their behaviour in order to avoid being conspicuous, effectively producing a 'chilling effect'" on their public actions (Taylor 77). Hidden cameras and other devices render all public space private because they allow the viewer to dominate the viewed, who have no recourse for open response to or correction of that domination.

Cruz 5

The possibility that all digital behavior—from accessing bank account information at an ATM to surfing the web—can be collected and used by unknown individuals can restrict an individual's activities. As more and more data is collected about our activities, both on and offline, advertisers are able to target individual consumers based on their behavior. This kind of surveillance turns daily activities like watching television and surfing the web into information collection sites that facilitate the profiling of individuals.

In our current age of constant data collection and increasing public surveillance, the topic of privacy should be of concern to everyone. However, when discussing the role of privacy in contemporary society, part of that discussion should be focused on the kind of privacy that should be protected, as well as the public space that will result from that protection. As Patricia Boling argues, public and private aren't terms whose definitions are "fixed and immune to change or criticism"; rather, they are "permeable realms of human life which change over time" (qtd. in Fairfield 13). It is our job to make sure that the forms which the public and private take in this new century support the equality of all citizens and do not allow injustice to evade public scrutiny.

Cruz 6

Works Cited

Eckersley, Peter. "PrivacyFinder.org: Search, but with Privacy." *Deeplinks*. Electronic Frontier Foundation, 25 Mar. 2008. Web. 30 Apr. 2009.

Fairfield, Paul. *Public/Private*. Lanham: Rowman, 2005. Print.

Jones, Helen. "Visible Rights: Watching Out for Women." *Surveillance and Society* 2 (2005): 589-93. Print.

Koskela, Hille. "'Cam Era'—the Contemporary Urban Panopticon." *Surveillance and Society* 1 (2003): 292-313. Print.

Lee, Jennifer. "Caught on Tape, Then Just Caught." *New York Times* 22 May 2005, final ed.: A33. Print.

Mieszkowski, Katharine. "We Are All Paparazzi Now." *Salon*. Salon, 25 Sep. 2003. Web. 22 Apr. 2009.

Story, Louise. "Internet Companies Know What You Are Looking For." *International Herald Tribune* 11 Mar. 2008: 1. *LexisNexis Academic*. Web. 21 Apr. 2009.

---. "Online Marketers Joining Internet Privacy Efforts." *New York Times* 31 Oct. 2007, final ed.: C1. Print.

Taylor, Nick. "State Surveillance and the Right to Privacy." *Surveillance and Society* 1 (2002): 66-85. Print.

Zaslow, Jeffrey. "If Tivo Thinks You Are Gay, Here's How to Set It Straight". *Wall Street Journal* 26 Nov. 2002: A1. *LexisNexis Academic*. Web. 16 Apr. 2009.

Center "Works Cited" on a new page. Alphabetize entries by the last names of the authors or by the first important word in the title if no author is listed.

Double-space all entries. Indent all but the first line in each entry five spaces.

FORMATTING THE WORKS-CITED LIST IN MLA STYLE

- **Begin the works-cited list on a new page.** Insert a page break with your word processor before you start the works-cited page.
- **Center "Works Cited" on the first line at the top of the page.**
- **Double-space all entries.**
- **Alphabetize each entry by the last name of the author or, if no author is listed, by the first content word in the title (ignore *a, an, the*).**
- **Indent all but the first line in each entry one-half inch (five spaces).**
- **Italicize the titles of books and periodicals.**
- **If an author has more than one entry, list the entries in alphabetical order by title. Use three hyphens in place of the author's name for the second and subsequent entries.**

  Murphy, Dervla. *Cameroon with Egbert*. Woodstock: Overlook, 1990. Print.

  ---. *Full Tilt: Ireland to India with a Bicycle*. London: Murray, 1965. Print.

- **Go through your paper to check that each source you have used is included in the works-cited list.**

15 APA Documentation

APA style is followed in the social sciences and education.

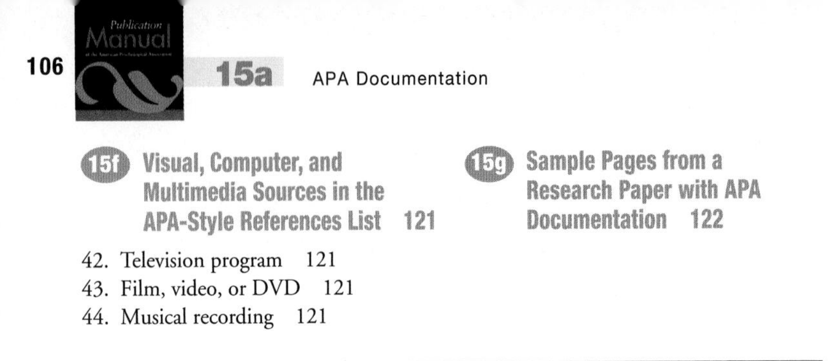

Social sciences disciplines, including government, linguistics, psychology, sociology, and education, frequently use the American Psychological Association (APA) documentation style. For a detailed treatment of APA style, consult the *Publication Manual of the American Psychological Association*, 5th ed. (2001) and the *APA Style Guide to Electronic References* (2007), available online.

15a The Elements of APA Documentation

APA style emphasizes the date of publication. When you cite an author's name in the body of your paper, always include the date of publication. Notice too that APA style includes the abbreviation for page (p.) in front of the page number. A comma separates each element of the citation.

> Zukin (2004) observes that teens today begin to shop for themselves at age 13 or 14, "the same age when lower-class children, in the past, became apprentices or went to work in factories" (p. 50).

When the author's name is not mentioned in the sentence, the reference will look like this:

> One sociologist notes that teens today begin to shop for themselves at age 13 or 14, "the same age when lower-class children, in the past, became apprentices or went to work in factories" (Zukin, 2004, p. 50).

The corresponding entry in the references list would be

Zukin, S. (2004). *Point of purchase: How shopping changed American culture*. New York: Routledge.

See page 124 for a sample references list.

15b Sample In-text Citations in APA Style

WHEN DO YOU NEED TO GIVE A PAGE NUMBER?

- Give the page number for all direct quotations.
- For electronic sources that do not provide page numbers, give the paragraph number when available. Use the abbreviation *para.* or the symbol ¶.
- You do *not* need to provide page numbers when paraphrasing or referring to ideas in other works.

1. Author named in your text

Influential sociologist Daniel Bell (1973) noted a shift in the United States to the "postindustrial society" (p. 3).

2. Author not named in your text

In 1997, the Gallup poll reported that 55% of adults in the United States think secondhand smoke is "very harmful," compared to only 36% in 1994 (Saad, 1997, p. 4).

3. Work by one author

(Bell, 1973, p. 3)

4. Work by two authors

(Suzuki & Irabu, 2002, p. 404)

5. Work by three to five authors

The authors' last names follow the order of the title page:

(Francisco, Vaughn, & Romano, 2001, p. 7)

Subsequent references can use the first name and *et al.*

(Francisco et al., 2001, p. 17)

6. Work by six or more authors

Use the first author's last name and *et al.* for all in-text references:

(Swallit et al., 2004, p. 49)

7. Work by a group or organization

Identify the group author in the text and place only the page number in parentheses:

The National Organization for Women (2001) observed that this "generational shift in attitudes towards marriage and childrearing" will have profound consequences (p. 325).

8. Work by an unknown author

Use a shortened version of the title (or the full title if it is short) in place of the author's name. Capitalize all key words in the title. If it is an article title, place it in quotation marks.

("Derailing the Peace Process," 2003, p. 44)

9. Two works by one author with the same copyright date

Assign the dates letters (*a*, *b*, etc.) according to their alphabetical arrangement in the references list.

> The majority of books written about coauthorship focus on partners of the same sex (Laird, 2001a, p. 351).

10. Two or more sources within the same sentence

Place each citation directly after the statement it supports.

> Some surveys report an increase in homelessness rates (Alford, 2004) while others chart a slight decrease (Rice, 2003a) . . .

11. Work quoted in another source

Name the work and give a citation for the secondary source.

> Saunders and Kellman's study (as cited in McAtee, Luhan, Stiles, & Buell, 1994)

12. Quotations 40 words or longer

Indent long quotations one-half inch and omit quotation marks. Note that the period appears before the parentheses following an indented "block" quote.

> Orlean (2001) has attempted to explain the popularity of the painter Thomas Kinkade:
>
> > People like to own things they think are valuable. . . . The high price of limited editions is part of their appeal; it implies that they are choice and exclusive, and that only a certain class of people will be able to afford them. (p. 128)

15c Books and Nonperiodical Sources in the APA-Style References List

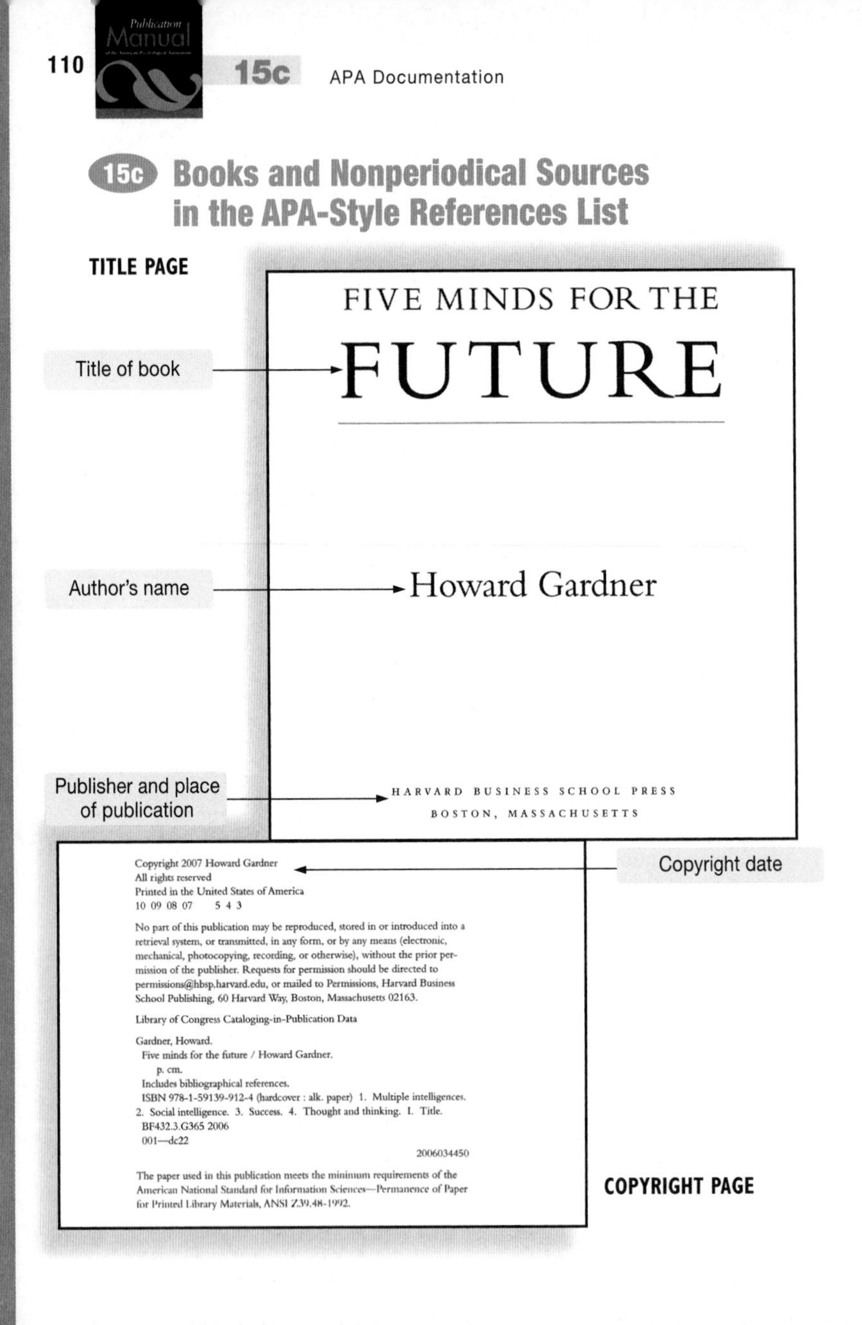

FIVE MINDS FOR THE

FUTURE

Howard Gardner

HARVARD BUSINESS SCHOOL PRESS
BOSTON, MASSACHUSETTS

Copyright 2007 Howard Gardner
All rights reserved
Printed in the United States of America
10 09 08 07 5 4 3

No part of this publication may be reproduced, stored in or introduced into a retrieval system, or transmitted, in any form, or by any means (electronic, mechanical, photocopying, recording, or otherwise), without the prior permission of the publisher. Requests for permission should be directed to permissions@hbsp.harvard.edu, or mailed to Permissions, Harvard Business School Publishing, 60 Harvard Way, Boston, Massachusetts 02163.

Library of Congress Cataloging-in-Publication Data

Gardner, Howard.
Five minds for the future / Howard Gardner.
p. cm.
Includes bibliographical references.
ISBN 978-1-59139-912-4 (hardcover : alk. paper) 1. Multiple intelligences.
2. Social intelligence. 3. Success. 4. Thought and thinking. I. Title.
BF432.3.G365 2006
001—dc22
2006034450

The paper used in this publication meets the minimum requirements of the American National Standard for Information Sciences—Permanence of Paper for Printed Library Materials, ANSI Z39.48-1992.

Gardner, H. (2007). *Five minds for the future.* Boston: Harvard
Business School Press.

AUTHOR'S OR EDITOR'S NAME

The author's last name comes first, followed by a comma and the author's initials.

If an editor, put the abbreviation *Ed*. in parentheses after the name:

Kavanagh, P. (Ed.).

BOOK TITLE

- Italicize the title.
- Capitalize only the first word, proper nouns, and the first word after a colon. Titles of books in APA style follow standard sentence capitalization.
- If the title is in a foreign language, copy it exactly as it appears on the title page.

YEAR OF PUBLICATION

- Give the year the work was copyrighted in parentheses.
- If no year of publication is given, write *n.d.* ("no date") in parentheses:

Smith, S. (n.d.).

- If it is a multivolume edited work published over a period of more than one year, put the span in parentheses:

Smith, S. (1999–2001).

PUBLICATION INFORMATION

Place of publication

- List the city without a state or country abbreviation for major cities known for publishing (New York, Boston).
- Add the state or country abbreviation for other cities (Foster City, CA). If the publisher is a university named for a state, omit the state abbreviation.
- If more than one city is given on the title page, list only the first.

Publisher's name

Do not shorten or abbreviate words like *University* or *Press*. Omit words such as *Co., Inc.,* and *Publishers*.

Sample references for books

13. Book by one author

Ball, E. (2000). *Slaves in the family.* New York: Ballantine Books.

For edited works, use the abbreviation *Ed.* in parentheses.

Kavanagh, P. (Ed.). (1969). *Lapped furrows.* New York: Hand Press.

14. Two or more books by the same author

Arrange according to the date, with the earliest publication first.

Jules, R. (2003). *Internal memos and other classified documents.* London: Hutchinson.

Jules, R. (2004). *Derelict cabinet.* London: Corgi-Transworld.

15. Book by two authors

Hardt, M., & Negri, A. (2000). *Empire.* Cambridge, MA: Harvard University Press.

For edited works, use *(Eds.)* after the names.

McClelland, D., & Eismann, K. (Eds.).

16. Book by three or more authors

The seventh and subsequent authors can be abbreviated to *et al.*

Anders, K., Child, H., Davis, K., Logan, O., Petersen, J., Tymes, J., et al.

17. Book by an unknown author

Survey of developing nations. (2003). New York: Justice for All Press.

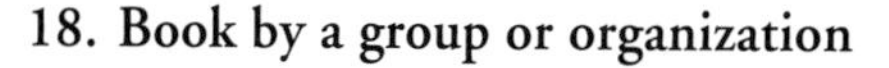

18. Book by a group or organization

When the author and publisher are identical, use the word *Author* as the name of the publisher.

Centers for Disease Control and Prevention. (2003). *Men and heart disease: An atlas of racial and ethnic disparities in mortality*. Atlanta, GA: Author.

19. Chapter in an edited collection

Howard, A. (1997). Labor, history, and sweatshops in the new global economy. In A. Ross (Ed.), *No sweat: Fashion, free trade, and the rights of garment workers* (pp. 151–172). New York: Verso.

20. Article in a reference work

Viscosity. (2001). *The Columbia encyclopedia* (6th ed.). New York: Columbia University Press.

21. Government document

U.S. Environmental Protection Agency. (2002). *Respiratory health effects of passive smoking: Lung cancer and other disorders.* (EPA Publication No. 600/6-90/006 F). Washington, DC: Author.

22. Religious or classical texts

Reference entries are not required for major classical works or the Bible, but in the first in-text citation, identify the edition used.

John 3.16 (Modern Phrased Version)

15d Periodical Sources in the APA-Style References List

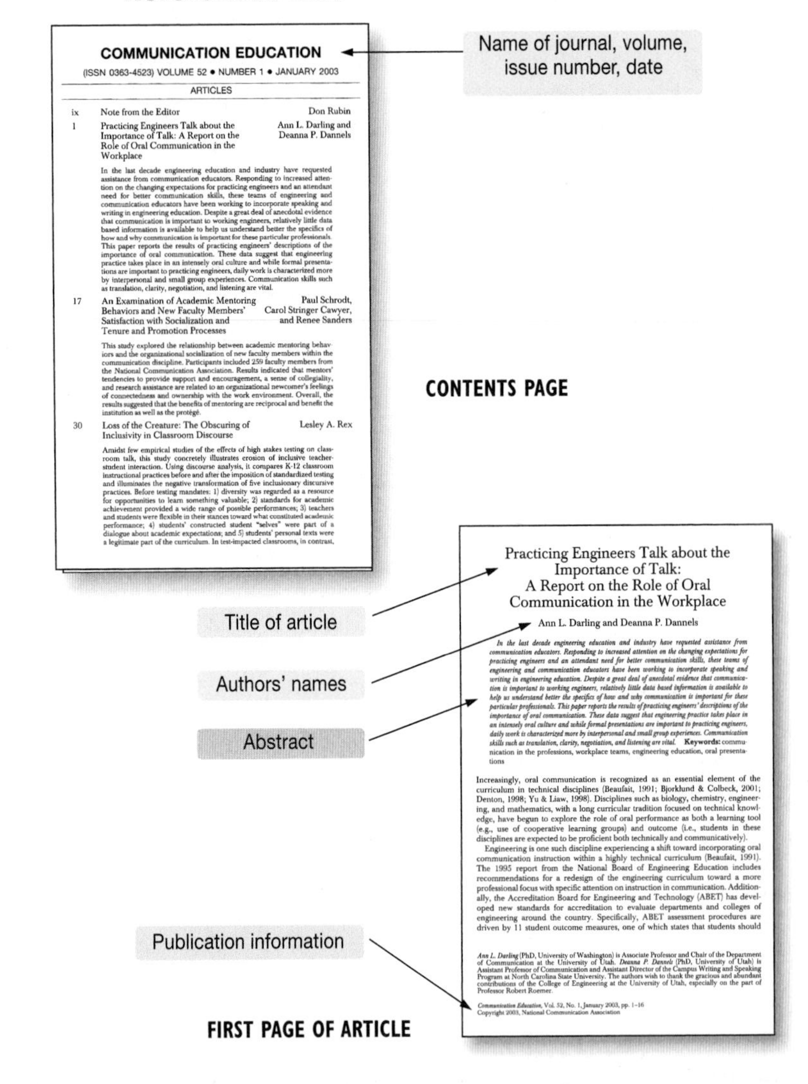

COMMUNICATION EDUCATION

(ISSN 0363-4523) VOLUME 52 • NUMBER 1 • JANUARY 2003

ARTICLES

Practicing Engineers Talk about the Importance of Talk: A Report on the Role of Oral Communication in the Workplace

Ann L. Darling and Deanna P. Dannels

In the last decade engineering education and industry have requested assistance from communication educators. Responding to increased attention on the changing expectations for practicing engineers and an attendant need for better communication skills, these teams of engineering and communication educators have been working to incorporate speaking and writing in engineering education. Despite a great deal of anecdotal evidence that communication is important to working engineers, relatively little data based information is available to help us understand better the specifics of how and why communication is important for these particular professionals. This paper reports the results of practicing engineers' descriptions of the importance of oral communication. These data suggest that engineering practice takes place in an intensely oral culture and while formal presentations are important to practicing engineers, daily work is characterized more by interpersonal and small group experiences. Communication skills such as translation, clarity, negotiation, and listening are vital. **Keywords:** communication in the professions, workplace teams, engineering education, oral presentations

Increasingly, oral communication is recognized as an essential element of the curriculum in technical disciplines (Beaufait, 1991; Bjorklund & Colbeck, 2001; Denton, 1998; Yu & Liaw, 1998). Disciplines such as biology, chemistry, engineering, and mathematics, with a long curricular tradition focused on technical knowledge, have begun to explore the role of oral performance as both a learning tool (e.g., use of cooperative learning groups) and outcome (i.e., students in these disciplines are expected to be proficient both technically and communicatively).

Engineering is one such discipline experiencing a shift toward incorporating oral communication instruction within a highly technical curriculum (Beaufait, 1991). The 1995 report from the National Board of Engineering Education includes recommendations for a redesign of the engineering curriculum toward a more professional focus with specific attention on instruction in communication. Additionally, the Accreditation Board for Engineering and Technology (ABET) has developed new standards for accreditation to evaluate departments and colleges of engineering around the country. Specifically, ABET assessment procedures are driven by 11 student outcome measures, one of which states that students should

Ann L. Darling (PhD, University of Washington) is Associate Professor and Chair of the Department of Communication at the University of Utah. *Deanna P. Dannels* (PhD, University of Utah) is Assistant Professor of Communication and Assistant Director of the Campus Writing and Speaking Program at North Carolina State University. The authors wish to thank the gracious and abundant contributions of the College of Engineering at the University of Utah, especially on the part of Professor Robert Roemer.

Communication Education, Vol. 52, No. 1, January 2003, pp. 1–16

Darling, A. L., & Dannels, D. P. (2003). Practicing engineers talk about the importance of talk: A report on the role of oral communication in the workplace. *Communication Education, 52,* 1–16.

AUTHOR'S NAME

The author's last name comes first, followed by the author's initials.

Join two authors' names with a comma and an ampersand.

DATE OF PUBLICATION

Give the year the work was published in parentheses.

Most popular magazines are paginated per issue. Include the full date, for example: (2008, June 24).

TITLE OF ARTICLE

- Do not use quotation marks. If there is a book title in the article title, italicize it.
- Titles of articles in APA style follow standard sentence capitalization.

PUBLICATION INFORMATION

Name of journal

- Italicize the journal name.
- All nouns, verbs, and pronouns, and the first word of the title are capitalized. Do not capitalize any article, preposition, or coordinating conjunction unless it is the first word of the title or subtitle.
- Put a comma after the journal name.

VOLUME, ISSUE, AND PAGE NUMBERS

- Italicize the volume number followed by a comma.
- See sample references 26 and 27 for more on different types of pagination.

Sample references for periodical sources

23. Article by one author

Kellogg, R. T. (2001). Competition for working memory among writing processes. *American Journal of Psychology, 114,* 175–192.

24. Article by multiple authors

Darling, A. L., & Dannels, D. P. (2003). Practicing engineers talk about the importance of talk: A report on the role of oral communication in the workplace. *Communication Education, 52,* 1–16.

25. Article by an unknown author

The net is where the kids are. (2003, May 10). *Business Week,* 44.

26. Article in a journal with continuous pagination

Engen, R., & Steen, S. (2000). The power to punish: Discretion and sentencing reform in the war on drugs. *American Journal of Sociology, 105,* 1357–1395.

27. Article in a journal paginated by issue

Davis, J. (1999). Rethinking globalisation. *Race and Class, 40*(2/3), 37–48.

28. Monthly publications

Barlow, J. P. (1998, January). Africa rising: Everything you know about Africa is wrong. *Wired,* 142–158.

29. Newspaper article

Hagenbaugh, B. (2005, April 25). Grads welcome an uptick in hiring. *USA Today,* p. A1.

15e Online Sources in the APA-Style References List

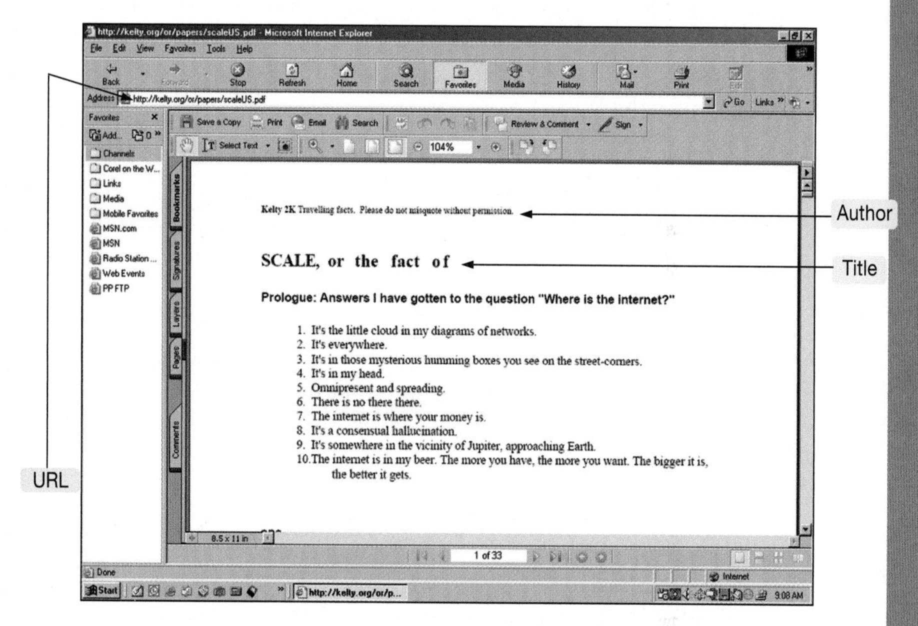

TITLES AND URLS IN APA-STYLE REFERENCES

Web sites are made up of many separate pages or articles. Each page on a Web site may or may not have a title. If you are citing a page or article that has a title, treat the title like an article in a periodical. No retrieval date is necessary if the content is not likely to be changed or updated.

Heiney, A. (2004). A gathering of space heroes. Retrieved from National Aeronautics and Space Administration Web site: http://www.nasa.gov/missions/shuttle/f_ahofpreview.html

Kelty, C. (2000). *Scale, or the fact of.* Retrieved January 2, 2007,

from http://kelty.org/or/papers/scaleUS.pdf

AUTHOR'S NAME OR ORGANIZATION

- If you do have an author or creator to cite, follow the rules for periodicals and books.
- If the only authority you find is a group or organization, list its name as the author.
- If the author is not identified, begin the reference with the title of the document.

DATES

First, list the date the site was produced or last revised (sometimes the copyright date) after the author.

Second, list the date of retrieval if the content may change or be updated. For published books and scholarly articles, do not list the date of retrieval.

TITLE OF PAGE OR ARTICLE

- Web sites are often made up of many separate pages or articles. If you are citing a page or article that has a title, treat the title like an article in a periodical. Otherwise, treat the name of the Web site itself as you would a book.
- The name of a Web site will usually be found on its index or home page. If you cannot find a link back to the home page, look at the address for clues.

URL

- Copy the address exactly as it appears in your browser window. You can even copy and paste the address into your text for greater accuracy.
- Break a URL at the end of a line before a mark of punctuation. Do not insert a hyphen.
- Note that there are no angle brackets around the URL and no period after it.

The *APA Style Guide to Electronic References* (2007) provides updated guidelines on how to cite online sources.

Sample references for online sources

30. Online publication by a known author

Carr, A. (2003, May 22). AAUW applauds senate support of title IX resolution. Retrieved from http://www.aauw.org/about/newsroom/press_releases/030522.cfm

31. Online publication by a group or organization

Girls Incorporated. (2003). Girls' bill of rights. Retrieved from http://www.girlsinc.org/gc/page.php?id=9

32. Online article with Digital Object Identifier (DOI) assigned

Because URLs frequently change, many scholarly publishers have begun to use a Digital Object Identifier (DOI), a unique alphanumeric string that is permanent. If a DOI is available, use the DOI instead of the URL. You may need to click on a button such as "Article" or "PubMed" to find the DOI. There is no need to list the database, the retrieval date, or the URL if the DOI is listed.

Erdfelder, E. (2008). Experimental psychology: Good news. *Experimental Psychology, 55*(1), 1-2. doi: 0.1027/1618-3169.55.1.1

33. Online article with no DOI assigned

Brown, B. (2004). The order of service: the practical management of customer interaction. *Sociological Research Online, 9*(4). Retrieved from http://www.socresonline.org.uk/9/4/brown.html

34. Article in an online newspaper

Erard, M. (2001, November 16). A colossal wreck. *Austin Chronicle.* Retrieved from http://www.austinchronicle.com/

35. Article in an online magazine

McClure, L. (2003, February 18). The Salon interview: Molly Ivins. *Salon*. Retrieved from http://www.salon.com

36. Document from a database

APA no longer requries listing the names of well-known databases. Include the name of the database only for hard-to-find books and other items. Give the DOI if it is available.

Holloway, J. D. (2004). Protecting practitioners' autonomy. *Monitor on Psychology, 35*(1), 30.

37. Online encyclopedia

Swing. (2002). In *Britannica Online*. Retrieved April 29, 2007, from http://www.britannica.com/

38. Blog entry

Albritton, C. (2004, May 19). Greetings from Baghdad. *Back to Iraq*. Retrieved from http://www.back-to-iraq.com/

39. Message posted to a newsgroup or discussion group

Use only messages that are archived and accessible by readers.

Truett, S. (2007, September 17). Where are the historians in popular political discourse? Message posted to http://www.h-net.org/~border/, archived at http://h-net.mus.edu/

40. Wiki

Because Wikis change frequently, the date of retrieval is important.

Mount Everest. (n.d.). Retrieved November 12, 2007, from Wikipedia: http://en.wikipedia.org/wiki/Mt._Everest

41. E-mail

E-mail sent from one individual to another should be cited as a personal communication. Personal communication is cited in text but not included in the reference list.

(S. Wilson, personal communication, August 18, 2007)

15f Visual, Computer, and Multimedia Sources in the APA-Style References List

42. Television program

Frolov, D., Schneider, A., Chase, D., & Weiner, M. (Writers), & Van Patten, T. (Director). (2007). Soprano home movies [Television series episode]. In D. Chase (Producer), *The sopranos*. New York: HBO.

43. Film, Video, or DVD

Miller, G. (Director). (2006). *Happy feet* [Motion picture]. United States: Warner Brothers.

44. Musical recording

Waits, T. (1980). Ruby's arms. On *Heartattack and vine* [CD]. New York: Elektra Entertainment.

15g Sample Pages from a Research Paper with APA Documentation

APA style uses a title page.

Include page header and page number, beginning with the title page.

Type the running head (the shortened title) for publication in all caps, flush left.

Center the title, name of author(s), and name of school.

Surveillanomics 1

Running head: SURVEILLANOMICS

Surveillanomics: The Need for Governmental Regulation of Video Surveillance

John M. Jones

The University of Texas at Austin

Continue to use the running head with the page number in the top right.

The abstract appears on a separate page with the title *Abstract*. An abstract may not exceed 120 words.

Do not indent the first line of the abstract.

Double-space the abstract.

Surveillanomics 2

Abstract

Because recent technological advances have made it possible to use surveillance video to gather information about private citizens, and because unregulated data-mining has made this information economically valuable, the collection and use of video surveillance data should be regulated by the government. This regulation, based on the model introduced by Taylor (2002), should mandate that all video surveillance must be in accordance with the law, have a legitimate objective, and be necessary for the maintenance of a free society. These guidelines would ensure that surveillance data could not be used for purposes other than those for which it was collected, and would make the primary concerns in debates over the use of surveillance democratic, not economic as they are now.

Surveillanomics: The Need for Governmental
Regulation of Video Surveillance

On September 5, 2005, the operators of the social networking site Facebook gave the service a facelift. One of the innovations they introduced was the "news feed" feature, which "automatically alerted users when their friends made changes to their online profiles," like changing personal details or adding new "friends" (Meredith, 2006). This service, which was automatically installed for all accounts, outraged users, 700,000 of whom formed the group "Students Against Facebook News Feeds." Before Facebook altered its implementation of this feature, the members of this group were preparing to protest the changes at the company's headquarters.

At first, this negative reaction by users took the company completely by surprise. As Schneier (2006) puts it, in their eyes, all they had done "was take available data and aggregate it in a novel way for what [they] perceived was [their] customers' benefit"; however, users realized that this change "made an enormous difference" in the way that their information could be aggregated, accessed, and distributed. In other words, although Facebook news feeds did nothing more than take information that was already publicly available and repackage it in a new form, this new information source was seen by users as a massive invasion of their privacy.

In light of this reaction, it is interesting to note that right now companies referred to as "data brokers" are creating

Give the full title at the beginning of the body of the report.

Specify 1-inch margins.

Indent each paragraph five to seven spaces (1/2″ on the ruler in the word processing program).

Include the date in parentheses when you mention authors in the text.

Surveilanomics 12

References

Center *References.*

Alphabetize entries by last name of the author.

Double-space all entries.

Indent all but the first line of each entry five spaces.

Go through your text and make sure that everything you have cited, except for personal communication, is in the list of references.

Koskela, H. (2000). 'The gaze without eyes': Video-surveillance and the changing nature of urban space. *Progress in Human Geography, 24*(2), 243–265.

Koskela, H. (2003). 'Cam era'—the contemporary urban panopticon. *Surveillance & Society, 1*(3), 292–313. Retrieved from http://www. surveillance-and-society.org

Lee, J. (2005, May 22). Caught on tape, then just caught: Private cameras transform police work. *The New York Times*. Retrieved from http://www.nytimes.com

Meredith, P. (2006, September 22). Facebook and the politics of privacy. *Mother Jones*. Retrieved from http://www.motherjones.com

Mieszkowski, K. (2003, September 25). We are all paparazzi now. *Salon*. Retrieved from http://archive.salon.com/tech /feature/2003/09/25/webcams/index.html

Nieto, M., Johnston-Dodds, K., & Simmons, C. W. (2002). *Public and private applications of video surveillance and biometric technologies*. Sacramento, CA: California Research Bureau, California State Library. Retrieved from http://www.library .ca.gov/CRB/02/06/02-006.pdf

O'Harrow, R. (2005). *No place to hide*. New York: Free Press.

Schneier, B. (2006, September 21). Lessons from the Facebook riots. *Wired News*. Retrieved from http://www.wired.com /news/columns/0,71815-0.html

16 CMS Documentation

CMS style offers flexibility and the option of using footnotes.

Writers in business, social sciences, fine arts, and humanities often use the *Chicago Manual of Style* (CMS) method of documentation. CMS guidelines allow writers a clear way of using footnotes and endnotes for citing the sources of quotations, summaries, and paraphrases. If you have further questions, consult the complete CMS style manual, *The Chicago Manual of Style,* 15th ed. (Chicago: University of Chicago Press, 2003).

16a The Elements of CMS Documentation

CMS style uses a superscript number directly after any quotation, paraphrase, or summary. This superscript number corresponds to either a footnote, which appears at the bottom of the page, or an endnote, which appears at the end of the text. Notes are numbered consecutively throughout the text.

> In *Southern Honor: Ethics and Behavior in the Old South,* Wyatt-Brown argues that "paradox, irony, and guilt have been three current words used by historians to describe white Southern life before the Civil War."[1]

Note

> 1. Bertram Wyatt-Brown, *Southern Honor: Ethics and Behavior in the Old South* (Oxford: Oxford University Press, 1983), 3.

Bibliography

> Wyatt-Brown, Bertram. *Southern Honor: Ethics and Behavior in the Old South.* Oxford: Oxford University Press, 1983.

Footnotes appear at the bottom of the page on which each citation appears. Begin your footnote four lines from the last line of text on the page. Footnotes are single-spaced, but you should double-space between notes.

Endnotes are compiled at the end of the text on a separate page entitled *Notes.* Center the title at the top of the page and list your endnotes in the order they appear within the text. The entire endnote section should be double-spaced—both within and between each entry.

Bibliography. Because footnotes and endnotes in CMS format contain complete citation information, a separate list of references is optional. This list of references can be called the *Bibliography* or, if it has only works referenced directly in your text, *Works Cited, Literature Cited,* or *References.* Generally, CMS bibliographies follow the MLA works-cited format.

See Section 16e for sample pages in CMS research paper format.

16b Books and Nonperiodical Sources in CMS Style

Note

1. Nell Irvin Painter, *Creating Black Americans: African-American History and Its Meanings, 1619 to the Present* (New York: Oxford University Press, 2006), 5.

Bibliography

Painter, Nell Irvin. *Creating Black Americans: African-American History and Its Meanings, 1619 to the Present.* New York: Oxford University Press, 2006.

AUTHOR'S OR EDITOR'S NAME

Note: the author's name is given in normal order.

Bibliography: give the author's name last name first. If an editor, put *ed.* after the name.

BOOK TITLE

Use the exact title, as it appears on the title page (not the cover).

Italicize the title.

Capitalize all nouns, verbs, adjectives, adverbs, and pronouns, and the first word of the title and subtitle.

PUBLICATION INFORMATION

In a note, the place of publication, publisher, and year of publication are in parentheses.

Place of publication

- Add the state's postal abbreviation or country when the city is not well known (Foster City, CA) or ambiguous (Cambridge, MA, or Cambridge, UK).
- If more than one city is given on the title page, use the first.

Publisher's name

- You may use acceptable abbreviations (e.g., Co. for Company).
- For works published prior to 1900, the place and date are sufficient.

Year of publication

- If no year of publication is given, write *n.d.* ("no date") in place of the date.
- If it is a multivolume edited work published over a period of more than one year, put the span of time as the year.

1. Book by one author

In a note, the author's name is given in normal order.

1. Thomas Friedman, *The World Is Flat: A Brief History of the Twenty-first Century* (New York: Farrar, Straus, and Giroux, 2005), 9.

In subsequent references, cite the author's last name only:

2. Friedman, 10.

If the reference is to the same work as the reference before it, you can use the abbreviation *Ibid.*:

3. Ibid., 10.

In the bibliography, give the author's name in reverse order.

Friedman, Thomas. *The World Is Flat: A Brief History of the Twenty-first Century*. New York: Farrar, Straus, and Giroux, 2005.

For edited books, put *ed.* after the name.

Chen, Kuan-Hsing, ed. *Trajectories: Inter-Asia Cultural Studies*. London: Routledge, 1998.

2. Book by two or three authors

In a note, put all authors' names in normal order. For subsequent references, give only the authors' last names:

4. McClelland and Eismann, 32.

In the bibliography, give second and third authors' names in normal order.

Hauser, Taylor, and June Kashpaw. *January Blues*. Foster City, CA: IDG Books, 2003.

3. Book by four or more authors

In a note, give the name of the first author listed, followed by *and others.*

5. Jacqueline Jones and others, *Created Equal: A Social and Political History of the United States* (New York: Longman, 2003), 243.

List all of the authors in the bibliography.

Jones, Jacqueline, Peter H. Wood, Elaine Taylor May, Thomas Borstelmann, and Vicki L. Ruiz. *Created Equal: A Social and Political History of the United States.* New York: Longman, 2003.

4. Book by a group or organization

Note

7. World Health Organization. *Advancing Safe Motherhood through Human Rights* (Geneva, Switzerland: WHO, 2001), 18.

Bibliography

World Health Organization. *Advancing Safe Motherhood through Human Rights*. Geneva, Switzerland: WHO, 2001.

5. A selection in an anthology or a chapter in an edited collection

Note

3. Renato Constantino, "Globalization and the South," in *Trajectories: Inter-Asia Cultural Studies,* ed. Kuan-Hsing Chen (London: Routledge, 1998), 57–64.

Bibliography

Constantino, Renato. "Globalization and the South." *In Trajectories: Inter-Asia Cultural Studies*, edited by Kuan-Hsing Chen, 57–64. London: Routledge, 1998.

6. Government document

Note

5. U.S. Department of Health and Public Safety, *Grade School Hygiene and Epidemics* (Washington, DC: GPO, 1998), 21.

Bibliography

U.S. Department of Health and Public Safety. *Grade School Hygiene and Epidemics*. Washington, DC: GPO, 1998.

7. Religious texts

Citations from religious texts appear in the notes but not in the bibliography. Give the version in parentheses in the first citation only.

Note

4. John 3:16 (King James Version).

Note

1. Michael Hutt, "A Nepalese Triangle: Monarchists, Maoists, and Political Parties," *Asian Affairs* 38 (2007): 11–22.

Bibliography

Hutt, Michael. "A Nepalese Triangle: Monarchists, Maoists, and Political Parties." *Asian Affairs* 38 (2007): 11–22.

AUTHOR'S OR EDITOR'S NAME

Note: the author's name is given in normal order.

Bibliography: give the author's last name first.

TITLE OF ARTICLE

- Put the title in quotation marks. If there is a title of a book within the title, italicize it.
- Capitalize nouns, verbs, adjectives, adverbs, and pronouns, and the first word of the title and subtitle.

PUBLICATION INFORMATION

Name of journal

- Italicize the name of the journal.
- Journal titles are normally not abbreviated in the arts and humanities unless the title of the journal is an abbreviation (*PMLA, ELH*).

Volume, issue, and page numbers

- Place the volume number after the journal title without intervening punctuation.
- For journals that restart pagination with each issue, list the issue number (preceded by a comma and *no.*) before the year.
- List the inclusive page numbers following the year (preceded by a colon).

Date

- The date or year of publication is given in parentheses after the volume number, or issue number if provided.

8. Article by one author

Note

1. Sumit Guha, "Speaking Historically: The Changing Voices of Historical Narration in Western India, 1400–1900," *American Historical Review* 109 (2004): 1084–98.

Bibliography

Guha, Sumit. "Speaking Historically: The Changing Voices of Historical Narration in Western India, 1400–1900." *American Historical Review* 109 (2004): 1084–98.

9. Article by two or three authors

Note

3. Pamela R. Matthews and Mary Ann O'Farrell, "Introduction: Whose Body?" *South Central Review* 18, no. 3–4 (Fall-Winter 2001): 1–5.

Bibliography

Matthews, Pamela R., and Mary Ann O'Farrell. "Introduction: Whose Body?" *South Central Review* 18, no. 3–4 (Fall-Winter 2001): 1–5.

10. Article by more than three authors

Note

5. Michael J. Thompson, Jorgen Christensen-Dalsgaard, Mark S. Miech, and Juir Thome, "The Internal Rotation of the Sun," *Annual Review of Astronomy and Astrophysics* 41 (2003): 599–643.

Bibliography

Thompson, Michael J., Jorgen Christensen-Dalsgaard, Mark S. Miesch, and Juri Toomre. "The Internal Rotation of the Sun." *Annual Review of Astronomy and Astrophysics* 41 (2003): 599–643.

11. Journals paginated by volume

Note

4. Susan Welsh, "Resistance Theory and Illegitimate Reproduction," *College Composition and Communication* 52 (2001): 553–73.

Bibliography

Welsh, Susan. "Resistance Theory and Illegitimate Reproduction." *College Composition and Communication* 52 (2001): 553–73.

12. Journals paginated by issue

Note

5. Tzvetan Todorov, "The New World Disorder," *South Central Review* 19, no. 2 (2002): 28–32.

Bibliography

Todorov, Tzvetan. "The New World Disorder." *South Central Review* 19, no. 2 (2002): 28–32.

13. Weekly and biweekly magazines

Note

5. Roddy Doyle, "The Dinner," *New Yorker*, February 5, 2001, 73.

Bibliography

Doyle, Roddy. "The Dinner." *New Yorker*, February 5, 2001, 73.

14. Newspaper article

1. Larry Kaplow and Tasgola Karla Bruner, "U.S.: Don't Let Taliban Forces Flee," *Austin American-Statesman*, November 20, 2001, final edition, sec. A.

16d Online Sources in CMS Style

15. Document or page from a Web site

To cite original content from within a Web site, include as many descriptive elements as you can: author of the page, title of the page, title and owner of the Web site, and the URL. Include the date accessed only if the site is time-sensitive or is frequently updated. If you cannot locate an individual author, the owner of the site can stand in for the author.

Note

11. National Organization for Women, "NOW History," http://www.now.org/history/history.html.

Bibliography

National Organization for Women. "NOW History." http://www.now.org.history/history.html.

CITING ONLINE SOURCES IN CMS STYLE

CMS advocates a style for citing online and electronic sources that is adapted from its style used for citing print sources. Titles of complete works are italicized. Quotation marks and other punctuation in citations for online sources should be used in the same manner as for print sources.

Access dates: CMS does not generally recommend the use of access dates, except in time-sensitive fields such as law or medicine.

Revision dates: Due to the inconsistency in the practice of Web sites stating the date of last revision, CMS also recommends against using revision dates in citations.

URLs: If a URL has to be broken at the end of a line, the line break should be made after a slash (/) or double slash (//) or before most other marks of punctuation. CMS does not advocate the use of angle brackets (<>) to enclose URLs.

For details not covered in this section, consult *The Chicago Manual of Style*, 15th ed., sections 17.4–17.15, "The Advent of Electronic Sources."

16. Online book

Note

12. Angelina Grimké, *Appeal to the Christian Women of the South* (New York: New York Anti-Slavery Society, 1836), http://history .furman.edu/~benson/docs/ grimke2. htm.

Bibliography

Grimké, Angelina. *Appeal to the Christian Women of the South.* New York: New York Anti-Slavery Society, 1836. http://history.furman.edu /~benson/docs/grimke2.htm.

17. Online article

Note

13. Emily Bazelon, "Little Geniuses," *Slate,* May 11, 2007, http://www.slate.com/id/2165995/.

Bibliography

Bazelon, Emily. "Little Geniuses." *Slate*, May 11, 2007. http://www.slate.com/id/2165995/.

18. Posting to a discussion list or group

To cite material from archived Internet forums, discussion groups, MOOs, or blogs, include the name of the post author, the name of the list or site, the date of the posting, and the URL. Limit your citation to notes or in-text citations.

16. Jason Marcel, post to U.S. Politics Online Today in Politics Forum, April 4, 2004, http://www.uspoliticsonline.com/forums/forumdisplay.php?f=24.

19. E-mail

Because personal e-mails are not available to the public, they are not usually listed in the bibliography.

Note

11. Erik Lynn Williams, e-mail message to author, August 12, 2007.

16e Sample Pages from a Research Paper with CMS Documentation

1

Jason Laker

Professor Bhatia

American History 102

January 9, 2008

The Electoral College: Does It Have a Future?

Until the presidential election of 2000, few Americans thought much about the Electoral College. It was something they had learned about in civics class and had then forgotten about as other, more pressing bits of information required their attention. In November 2000, however, the Electoral College took center stage and sparked an argument that continues today: Should the Electoral College be abolished?

The founding fathers established the Electoral College as a compromise between elections by Congress and those by popular vote.[1] The College consists of a group of electors who meet to vote for the president and vice president of the United States. The electors are nominated by political parties within each state and the number each state gets relates to the state's congressional delegation.[2] The process and the ideas behind it sound simple, but the actual workings of the Electoral College remain a mystery to many Americans.

The complicated nature of the Electoral College is one of the reasons why some people want to see it abolished.

4

Notes

1. Lawrence D. Longley and Neal R. Peirce, *The Electoral College Primer 2000* (New Haven: Yale University Press, 1999).

2. Office of the Federal Register, "A Procedural Guide to the Electoral College," Electoral College Home page, http://www.archives.gov/federal-register/electoral-college/procedural_guide.html.

3. Nicola Maaser and Stefan Napel, "Equal Representation in Two-Tier Voting Systems," *Social Choice and Welfare* 28 (2007): 401–20.

4. Avagara, *EC: The Electoral College Webzine*, http://www.avagara.com/e_c/.

5. Robert W. Bennett, *Taming the Electoral College* (Palo Alto, CA: Stanford University Press, 2006), 246.

5

Bibliography

Avagara. EC: The Electoral College Webzine. http://www.avagara.com/e_c/.

Bennett, Robert W. Taming the Electoral College. Palo Alto, CA: Stanford University Press, 2006.

17 CSE Documentation

CSE style applies for all scientific disciplines.

Within the disciplines of the natural and applied sciences, citation styles are highly specialized. Many disciplines follow the guidelines of particular journals or style manuals within their individual fields. Widely followed by writers in the sciences is the comprehensive guide published by the Council of Science Editors: *Scientific Style and Format: The CSE Manual for Authors, Editors, and Publishers,* 7th ed. (2006).

The preferred documentation system in CSE places references in the body of the text marked by a superscript number placed inside punctuation. For example:

> Cold fingers and toes are common circulatory problems found in most heavy cigarette smokers[1].

This number corresponds to a numbered entry on the CSE source list, titled *References.*

The CSE References page lists all sources cited in the paper. To create a CSE References page, follow these guidelines:

1. Title your page "References," and center this title at the top of the page.
2. Double-space the entire References page, both within and between citations.
3. List citations in the order they appear in the body of the paper. Begin each citation with its citation number, followed by a period, flush left.
4. Authors are listed by last name, followed by initials. Capitalize only first words and proper nouns in cited titles. Titles are not underlined, and articles are not placed in quotations. Names of journals should be abbreviated where possible.
5. Cite publication year, and volume or page numbers if applicable.

17a In-text References in CSE Style

CSE documentation of sources does not require the names of authors in the text but only a number that refers to the References list at the end.

> In 1997, the Gallup poll reported that 55% of adults in the United States think secondhand smoke is "very harmful," compared to only 36% in 1994[1].

The superscript(1) refers to the first entry on the References list, where readers will find a complete citation for this source.

What if you need more than one citation in a passage?

If the numbers are consecutive, separate with a dash. If nonconsecutive, use a comma.

> The previous work[1, 3, 5–8, 11]

17b Books and Nonperiodical Sources in CSE-Style References

1. Nance JJ. What goes up: the global assault on our atmosphere. New York (NY): Morrow; 1991. 324 p.

AUTHOR'S OR EDITOR'S NAME

The author's last name comes first, followed by the initials of the author's first name and middle name (if provided). If an editor, put the word *editor* after the name.

BOOK TITLE

- Do not italicize or underline titles.
- Capitalize only the first word and proper nouns.

PUBLICATION INFORMATION

Year of publication

- The year comes after the other publication information. It follows a semicolon.
- If it is a multivolume edited work, published over a period of more than one year, give the span of years.

Page numbers

- When citing an entire book, give the total number of pages: *324 p.*
- When citing part of a book, give the page range for the selection: *p. 60–90*.

Sample references

1. Book by one author/editor

2. Minger TJ, editor. Greenhouse glasnost: the crisis of global warming. New York (NY): Ecco; 1990. 292 p.

2. Book by two or more authors/editors

3. O'Day DH, Horgen PA, editors. Sexual interactions in eukaryotic microbes. New York (NY): Academic; 1981. 407 p.

3. Book by a group or organization

4. IAEA. Manual on radiation haematology. Vienna (Austria): IAEA; 1971. 430 p.

4. A single chapter written by the same author as the book

6. Ogle M. All the modern conveniences: American household plumbing, 1840–1890. Baltimore (MD): Johns Hopkins University Press; 2000. Convenience embodied; p. 60–92.

5. A selection in an anthology or a chapter in an edited collection

7. Kraft K, Baines DM. Computer classrooms and third grade development. In: Green MD, editor. Computers and early development. New York (NY): Academic; 1997. p. 168–79.

6. Technical and research reports

9. Austin A, Baldwin R, editors. Faculty collaboration: enhancing the quality of scholarship and teaching. ASCHE-ERIC Higher Education Report No. 7. Washington (DC): George Washington University; 1991.

17c Periodical Sources in CSE-Style References

1. Bohannon J. Climate change: IPCC report lays out options for taming greenhouse gases. Science. 2007;316(5826):812–814.

AUTHOR'S NAME

The author's last name comes first, followed by the initials of the author's first name and middle name (if provided).

TITLE OF ARTICLE

- Do not italicize or underline titles.
- Capitalize only the first word and proper nouns.

PUBLICATION INFORMATION

Name of journal

- Do not abbreviate single-word titles. Abbreviate multiple-word titles according to the National Information Standards Organization (NISO) list of serials.
- Capitalize the journal title, even if abbreviated.

Date of publication, volume, and issue numbers

- Include the issue number inside parentheses if it is present in the document. Leave no spaces between these items.

7. Article by one author

1. Board J. Reduced lodging for soybeans in low plant population is related to light quality. Crop Science. 2001;41:379–387.

8. Article by two or more authors/editors

2. Simms K, Denison D. Observed interactions between wild and domesticated mixed-breed canines. J Mamm. 1997;70:341–342.

9. Article by a group or organization

4. Center for Science in the Public Interest. Meat labeling: help! Nutrition Action Health Letter: 2. 2001 Apr 1.

10. Article with no identifiable author

Use [Anonymous].

17d Online Sources in CSE-Style References

11. Online journal articles

2. Schunck CH, Shin Y, Schirotzek A, Zwierlein MW, Ketterle A. Pairing without superfluidity: the ground state of an imbalanced fermi mixture. Science [Internet]. 2007 [cited 2007 Jun 15]; 316(5826):867–870. Available from: http://www.sciencemag.org/cgi/content/full/3165826/867/DC1

12. Scientific databases on the Internet

3. Comprehensive Large Array-data Stewardship System [Internet]. 2007. Release 4.2. Silver Spring (MD): National Environmental Satellite, Data, and Information Service (US). [updated 2007 May 2; cited 2007 May 14]. Available from: http://www.class.noaa.gov/saa/products/welcome

PART 4

Style and Language

18 Write with Power

Learn how to write an efficient sentence.

In photographs

You imagine actions when subjects are captured in motion.

In writing

Your readers expect actions to be expressed in verbs:
gallop, canter, trot, run, sprint, dash, bound, thunder, tear away.

In photographs

Viewers interpret the most prominent person or thing as the subject—what the photograph is about.

In writing

Readers interpret the first person or thing they meet in a sentence as what the sentence is about (the jockey, the horse). They expect that person or thing to perform the action expressed in the verb.

18a Recognize Active and Passive Voice

In the **active voice** the subject of the sentence is the actor. In the **passive voice** the subject is being acted upon.

Active **Leonardo da Vinci** painted *Mona Lisa* between 1503 and 1506.

Passive ***Mona Lisa*** was painted by Leonardo da Vinci between 1503 and 1506.

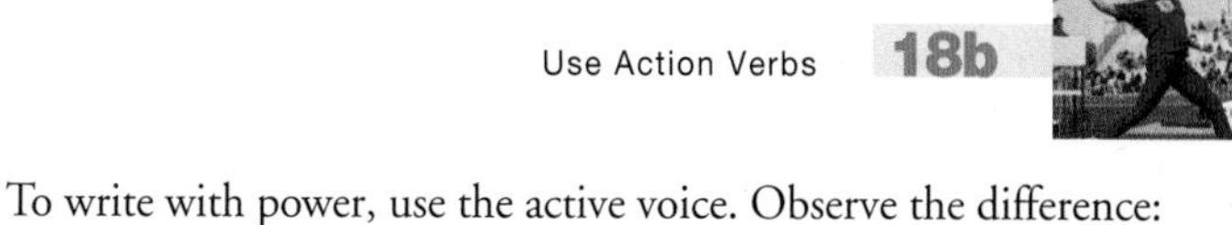

To write with power, use the active voice. Observe the difference:

Passive The pear tree in the front yard **was demolished** by the unexpected storm.

Active The unexpected storm **demolished** the pear tree in the front yard.

18b Use Action Verbs

Where are the action words in the following sentences?

> In August 1996, Tiger Woods was a new professional golfer with the slogan "Hello world." He was the winner of two events in the next three months and was a qualifier for the PGA Tour Championship. The following April, Woods was the winner of The Masters by a record margin of twelve strokes.

No action words here! The passage describes a series of actions, yet the only verbs are forms of *be (was, were).* Think about what the actions are and choose powerful verbs that express those actions.

> In August 1996, Tiger Woods **announced** "Hello world," launching his career as a professional golfer. He **won** two events in the next three months and **qualified** for the PGA Tour Championship. The following April, Woods **obliterated** the field to win his first major tournament, The Masters, by a record margin of twelve strokes.

Many sentences contain words that express action, but those words are nouns instead of verbs. Often the nouns can be changed into verbs. For example:

> The arson unit ~~conducted an investigation of~~ **investigated** the mysterious fire.
>
> The committee ~~had a debate over~~ **debated** how best to spend the surplus funds.

Notice that changing nouns into verbs also eliminates unnecessary words.

18c Find Agents

The **agent** is the person or thing that does the action. Powerful writing puts the agents in sentences.

Focus on people

Read the following sentence aloud:

> The use of a MIDI keyboard for playing the song will facilitate capturing it in digital form on our laptop for the subsequent purpose of uploading it to our Web site.

It sounds dead, doesn't it? Putting people into the sentence makes it come alive:

> By playing the song on a MIDI keyboard, we can record the digitized sound on our laptop and then upload it to our Web site.

Including people makes your writing more emphatic. Most readers relate better to people than to abstractions. Putting people in your sentences also introduces active verbs because people do things.

Identify characters

If people are not your subject, then keep the focus on other types of characters.

Without characters	The celebration of Martin Luther King Day had to be postponed because of inclement weather.
With characters	A severe ice storm forced the city to postpone the Martin Luther King Day celebration.

18d Vary Your Sentences

Read the following passage.

> On the first day Garth, Jim, and I paddled fourteen miles down Johnstone Strait. We headed down the strait about five more miles to Robson Bight. It is a famous scratching place for orcas. The Bight is a small bay. We paddled out into the strait so we could see the entire Bight. There were no orcas inside. By this time we were getting tired. We were hungry. The clouds assumed a wintry dark thickness. The wind was kicking up against us. Our heads were down going into the cold spray.

The subject matter is interesting, but the writing isn't. The passage is a series of short sentences, one after the other. When you have too many short sentences one after the other, try combining a few of them.

The result of combining some (but not all) short sentences is a paragraph whose sentences match the interest of the subject.

> On the first day Garth, Jim, and I paddled fourteen miles down Johnstone Strait. We headed down the strait about five more miles to Robson Bight, a small bay known as a famous scratching place for orcas. We paddled out into the strait so we could see the entire Bight, but there were no orcas inside. By this time we were tired and hungry, the clouds had assumed a wintry dark thickness, and the wind was kicking up against us—our heads dropped going into the cold spray.

19 Write Concisely

Put your writing on a diet and lose excess words.

 19a Eliminate Unnecessary Words

Clutter creeps into our lives every day. Clutter also creeps into writing through unnecessary words, inflated constructions, and excessive jargon.

> **In regards to** the Web site, the content is **pretty** successful in **consideration of** the topic. The site is **fairly** good **writing-wise** and is **very** unique in telling you how to adjust the rear derailleur one step at a time.

The words in **red** are clutter. Get rid of the clutter. You can say the same thing with half the words and gain more impact as a result.

> The well-written Web site on bicycle repair provides step-by-step instructions on adjusting your rear derailleur.

Redundancy

Some words act as modifiers, but when you look closely at them, they repeat the meaning of the word they pretend to modify. Have you heard someone refer to a *personal friend*? Aren't all friends personal? Likewise, you may have heard expressions such as *red in color, small in size, round in shape,* or *honest truth.* Imagine *red* not referring to color or *round* not referring to shape.

19b Reduce Wordy Phrases

Many inexperienced writers use phrases like "It is my opinion that" or "I think that" to begin sentences. These phrases are deadly to read. If you find them in your prose, cut them. Unless a writer is citing a source, we assume that the ideas are the writer's.

Coaches are among the worst at using many words for what could be said in a few:

> After much deliberation about Brown's future in football with regard to possible permanent injuries, I came to the conclusion that it would be in his best interest not to continue his pursuit of playing football again.

The coach might have said simply:

> Because Brown risks permanent injury if he plays football again, I decided to release him from the team.

Perhaps the coach wanted to sound impressive, authoritative, or thoughtful. But the result is the opposite. Speakers and writers who impress us are those who use words efficiently.

COMMON ERRORS

Empty intensifiers

Intensifiers modify verbs, adjectives, and other adverbs, and they are often overused. One of the most overused intensifiers is *very*. Take the following sentence as an example:

> Her clothing style was **very unique.**

(Continued on next page)

COMMON ERRORS (continued)

If something is unique, it is one of a kind. The word *very* doesn't make something more than unique.

> Her clothing style was **unique**.
>
> *Or*
>
> Her clothing style was **strange**.

Very and *totally* are but two of a list of empty intensifiers that can usually be eliminated with no loss of meaning. Other empty intensifiers include *absolutely, awfully, definitely, incredibly, particularly,* and *really.*

Remember: When you use *very, totally,* or another intensifier before an adjective or adverb, always ask yourself whether there is a more accurate adjective or adverb you could use instead to express the same thought.

WORDY PHRASES

Certain stock phrases plague writing in the workplace, in the media, and in academia. Many can be replaced by one or two words with no loss in meaning.

Wordy	Concise
at this point in time	now
due to the fact that	because
for the purpose of	for
have the ability to	can
in order to	to
in spite of the fact that	although
in the event that	if
met with her approval	she approved

19c Simplify Tangled Sentences

Long sentences can be graceful and forceful. Such sentences, however, often require several revisions before they achieve elegance. Too often long sentences reflect wandering thoughts that the writer did not bother to go back and sort out. Two of the most important strategies for untangling long sentences are described in Chapter 18: using active verbs (Section 18b) and naming your agents (Section 18c). Here are some other strategies.

Revise expletives

Expletives are empty words that can occupy the subject position in a sentence. The most frequently used expletives are *there is, there are,* and *it is.*

Wordy There were several important differences between the positions raised by the candidates in the debate.

To simplify the sentence, find the agent and make it the subject.

Revised The two candidates raised several important differences between their positions in the debate.

A few kinds of sentences—for example, *It is raining*—do require you to use an expletive. In most cases, however, expletives add unnecessary words, and sentences will read better without them.

Use positive constructions

Sentences become wordy and hard to read when they include two or more negatives such as the words *no, not,* and *nor,* and the prefixes *un-* and *mis-*. For example:

Difficult A not uncommon complaint among employers of new college graduates is that they cannot communicate effectively in writing.

Revised Employers frequently complain that new college graduates cannot write effectively.

Even Simpler Employers value the rare college graduate who can write well.

Phrasing sentences positively usually makes them more economical. Moreover, it makes your style more forceful and direct.

Simplify sentence structure

Long sentences can be hard to read, not because they are long but because they are convoluted and hide the relationships among ideas. Take the following sentence as an example.

> When the cessation of eight years of hostility in the Iran–Iraq war occurred in 1988, it was not the result of one side's defeating the other but the exhaustion of both after losing thousands of people and much of their military capability.

This sentence is hard to read. To rewrite sentences like this one, find the main ideas, then determine the relationships among them.

After examining the sentence, you decide there are two key ideas:

1. Iran and Iraq stopped fighting in 1988 after eight years.
2. Both sides were exhausted from losing people and equipment.

Next ask what the relationship is between the two ideas. When you identify the key ideas, the relationship is often obvious; in this case (2) is the cause of (1). Thus the word you want to connect the two ideas is *because.*

> Iran and Iraq stopped fighting after eight years of an indecisive war **because** both sides had lost thousands of people and most of their equipment.

The revised sentence is both clearer and more concise, reducing the number of words from forty-two to twenty-five.

20 Write with Emphasis

Make your key ideas stand out and not get lost.

Photographs and writing gain energy when key ideas are emphasized.

In visuals

Photographers create emphasis by composing the image to direct the attention of the viewer. Putting people and objects in the foreground and making them stand out against the background gives them emphasis.

In writing

Writers have many tools for creating emphasis. Writers can design a page to gain emphasis by using headings, white space, type size, color, and boldfacing. Just as important, learning the craft of structuring sentences will empower you to give your writing emphasis.

20a Manage Emphasis Within Sentences

Put your main ideas in main clauses

Placing more important information in main clauses and less important information in subordinate clauses emphasizes what is important.

In the following paragraph all the sentences are main clauses:

> Lotteries were common in the United States before and after the American Revolution. They eventually ran into trouble. They were run by private companies. Sometimes the companies took off with the money. They didn't pay the winners.

This paragraph is grammatically correct, but it does not help the reader understand which pieces of information the author wants to emphasize. Combining the simple sentences into main and subordinate clauses and phrases can significantly improve the paragraph.

First, identify the main ideas:

> Lotteries were common in the United States before and after the American Revolution. They eventually ran into trouble.

These ideas can be combined into one sentence:

> Lotteries were common in the United States before and after the American Revolution, but they eventually ran into trouble.

Now think about the relationship of the three remaining sentences to the main ideas. Those sentences explain why lotteries ran into trouble; thus the relationship is *because.*

> Lotteries were common in the United States before and after the American Revolution, but they eventually ran into trouble **because** they were run by private companies that sometimes took off with the money instead of paying the winners.

Put key ideas at the beginning and end of sentences

Read these sentences aloud:

1. *Courage Under Fire* and *Good Will Hunting*, films marking the actor's transition from teen idol to adult actor, starred **Matt Damon**.

2. Films such as *Courage Under Fire* and *Good Will Hunting*, both starring **Matt Damon**, helped the actor make the difficult transition from teen idol to adult actor.

3. **Matt Damon** made the difficult transition from teen idol to adult actor, starring in films such as *Courage Under Fire* and *Good Will Hunting*.

Most readers pay closest attention to the words at the beginning and end of sentences. Usually at the front of a sentence is what is known: the topic. At the end is the new information about the topic. Subordinate information is in the middle. If a paragraph is about Matt Damon, we would not expect the writer to choose sentence 2 over 1 or 3. In sentence 2 Damon is buried in the middle.

20b Forge Links Across Sentences

When your writing maintains a focus of attention across sentences, the reader can distinguish the important ideas and how they relate to each other. To achieve this coherence, you need to control which ideas occupy the positions of greatest emphasis. The words you repeat from sentence to sentence act as links.

Link sentences from front to front

In front-to-front linkage, the subject of the sentence remains the focus from one sentence to the next. In the following sequence, sentences 1 through 5 are all about Matt Damon. The subject of each sentence refers to the first sentence with the pronouns *he* and *his*.

1 Matt Damon was born in 1970 and grew up in Boston.

2 His first movie role was a one-line part in *Mystic Pizza* with Julia Roberts in 1988.

3 He dropped out of Harvard twelve credits short of graduating to pursue his acting career full time.

4 His first major role was that of a Gulf War vet-turned-heroin-addict in *Courage Under Fire* in 1996.

5 Since then he has frequently starred with his real-life best friend, Ben Affleck.

Each sentence adds more information about the repeated topic, Matt Damon.

Link sentences from back to front

In back-to-front linkage, the new information at the end of the sentence is used as the topic of the next sentence. Back-to-front linkage allows new material to be introduced and commented on.

1 Matt Damon's one-line part in *Mystic Pizza* was his first film role.

2 Hollywood film brokers recognized in *Chasing Amy* the potential of pairing Damon with his childhood friend Ben Affleck.

3 Affleck and Damon next wrote the screenplay for *Good Will Hunting*, in which they co-star.

Back-to-front linkage is useful when ideas need to be advanced quickly, as when you are telling stories. Rarely, however, will you use either front-to-front linkage or back-to-front linkage continuously throughout a piece of writing. Use front-to-front linkage to add more information and back-to-front linkage to move the topic along.

Check the links between your sentences to find any gaps that will cause your readers to stumble.

20c Use Parallel Structure with Parallel Ideas

What if Patrick Henry had written "Give me liberty or I prefer not to live"? Would we remember those words today? We remember the words he did use: "Give me liberty or give me death." Writers who use parallel structure often create memorable sentences.

Use parallelism with *and, or, nor, but*

When you join elements at the same level with coordinating conjunctions, including *and, or, nor, yet, so, but,* and *for,* normally you should use parallel grammatical structure for these elements.

Awkward

In today's global economy, **the method of production and where factories are located** has become relatively unimportant in comparison to **the creation of new concepts and marketing those concepts.**

Parallel

In today's global economy, how goods are made and where they are produced has become relatively unimportant in comparison to creating new concepts and marketing those concepts.

Use parallelism with *either/or, not only/but*

Make identical in structure the parts of sentences linked by correlative conjunctions: *either . . . or, neither . . . nor, not only . . . but also, whether . . . or.*

Awkward

Purchasing the undeveloped land **not only** gives us a new park **but also** it is something that our children will benefit from in the future.

Parallel

Purchasing the undeveloped land will **not only** give our city a new park **but will** also leave our children a lasting inheritance.

The more structural elements you match, the stronger the effect that parallelism will achieve.

COMMON ERRORS

Faulty parallel structure

When writers neglect to use parallel structure, the result can be jarring. Reading your writing aloud will help you catch problems in parallelism. Read this sentence aloud:

> At our club meeting we identified problems in **finding** new members, **publicizing** our activities, and **maintenance** of our Web site.

The end of the sentence does not sound right because the parallel structure is broken. We expect to find another verb + *ing* following *finding* and *publicizing*. Instead, we run into *maintenance,* a noun. The problem is easy to fix: Change the noun to the *-ing* verb form.

> At our club meeting we identified problems in finding new members, publicizing our activities, and **maintaining** our Web site.

Remember: Use parallel structure for parallel ideas.

21 Find the Right Words

Use precise language to express your ideas effectively.

21a Be Aware of Levels of Formality

While you may get plenty of practice in informal writing—emails and notes to friends and family members—mastering formal writing is essential in academic and professional settings. How formal or informal should your writing be? That depends on your audience and the writing task at hand.

DECIDE HOW FORMAL YOUR WRITING SHOULD BE

- Who is your audience?
- What is the occasion?
- What level of formality is your audience accustomed to in similar situations?
- What impression of yourself do you want to give?

Colloquialisms

Colloquialisms are words or expressions that are used informally, often in conversation but less often in writing.

> I'm not happy with my grades, but that's the way the cookie crumbles.
>
> Liz is always running off at the mouth about something.
>
> I enjoyed the restaurant, but it was nothing to write home about.

In academic and professional writing, colloquialisms often suggest a flippant attitude, carelessness, or even thoughtlessness. Sometimes colloquialisms can be used for ironic or humorous effect, but as a general rule, if you want to be taken seriously, avoid using them.

Avoiding colloquialisms does not mean, however, that you should use big words when small ones will do as well, or that you should use ten words instead of two. Formality does not mean being pretentious or wordy.

Wordy

> In this writer's opinion, one could argue that the beaches on the west coast of Florida are far superior in every particular to their counterparts on the east coast.

Better

> I think Florida's west coast beaches are better in every way than those on the east coast.

Slang

The most conspicuous kind of language that is usually avoided in formal writing is slang. The next time a friend talks to you, listen closely to the words he or she uses. Chances are you will notice several words that you probably would not use in a college writing assignment. Slang words are created by and for a particular group—even if that group is just you and your friend.

> The party was **bumpin** with all my **peeps**.
>
> Joey's new **ride** is totally **pimped** out.

Slang is used to indicate membership in a particular group, and usually to avoid others. But because slang excludes readers who are not members of the group, it is best avoided in academic writing.

21b Be Aware of Denotation and Connotation

Words have both literal meanings, called **denotations**, and associated meanings, called **connotations**. The contrast is evident in words that mean roughly the same thing but have different connotations. For example, some people are set in their opinions, a quality that can be described positively as *persistent, firm,* and *steadfast* or negatively as *stubborn, bull-headed,* and *close-minded.*

In college and professional writing, writers are expected not to rely on the connotations of words to make important points. For example, the statement *It's only common sense to have good schools* carries high positive connotations. Most people believe in common sense, and most people want good schools. What is common sense for one person, however, is not common sense for another; how a good school is defined varies greatly. You have an obligation in college writing to support any judgment with evidence.

21c Use Specific Language

Be precise

Effective writing conveys information clearly and precisely. Words such as *situation, sort, thing, aspect,* and *kind* often signal undeveloped or even lazy thinking.

Vague The violence aspect determines how video games are rated.

Better The level of violence determines how video games are rated.

When citing numbers or quantities, be as exact as possible. A precise number, if known, is always better than slippery words like *several* or *many,* which some writers use to cloak the fact that they don't know the quantity in question.

Use a dictionary

There is no greater tool for writers than the dictionary. Always have a dictionary handy when you write—either a book or an online version—and get into the habit of using it. In addition to checking spelling, you can find additional meanings of a word that perhaps you had not considered, and you can find the etymology—the origins of a word. In many cases knowing the etymology of a word can help you use it to better effect. For example, if you want to argue that universities as institutions have succeeded because they bring people together in contexts that prepare them for their lives after college, you might point out the etymology of *university. University* can be traced back to the late Latin word *universitas,* which means "society or guild," thus emphasizing the idea of a community of learning.

21d Write to Be Inclusive

While the conventions of inclusiveness change continually, three guidelines for inclusive language toward all groups remain constant:

- Do not point out people's differences unless those differences are relevant to your argument.
- Call people whatever they prefer to be called.
- When given a choice of terms, choose the more accurate one. (*Vietnamese,* for example, is preferable to *Asian.*)

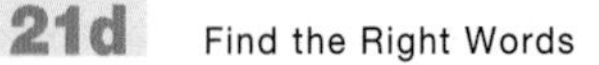

Be inclusive about gender

Don't use masculine nouns and pronouns to refer to both men and women. *He, his, him, man,* and *mankind* are outmoded and inaccurate terms for both genders. Eliminate gender bias by using the following tips:

- Don't say *boy* when you can say *child.*
- Use *men and women* or *people* instead of *man.*
- Use *humanity* or *humankind* in place of *mankind.*

Eliminating *he, his,* and *him* when referring to both men and women is more complicated. Many readers consider *he/she* to be an awkward alternative. Try one of the following instead:

- Make the noun and its corresponding pronoun plural. The pronoun will change from *he, him,* or *his* to *they, them,* or *theirs.*

Biased Masculine Pronouns

An undercover agent won't reveal **his** identity, even to other agents, if **he** thinks it will jeopardize the case.

Better

Undercover agents won't reveal **their** identities, even to other agents, if **they** think it will jeopardize the case.

- Replace the pronoun with an article (*the, a,* or *an*)

Biased Masculine Pronoun

Each prospective driving instructor must pass a state test before receiving **his** license.

Better

Each prospective driving instructor must pass a state test before receiving **a** license.

Professional titles that indicate gender—*chairman, waitress*—falsely imply that the gender of the person doing the job changes the essence of the job being done. Terms like *woman doctor* and *male nurse* imply that a

woman working as a doctor and a man working as a nurse are out of the ordinary. Instead, write simply *doctor* and *nurse.*

Be inclusive about race and ethnicity

Use the terms for racial and ethnic groups that the groups use for themselves. Use *black* to write about members of the Black Coaches' Association and *African American* to write about members of the Society for African American Brotherhood.

If you are still in doubt, err on the side of specificity. For instance, while *Latino(a), Hispanic,* and *Chicano(a)* are all frequently accepted terms for many people, choosing a term that identifies a specific country (*Mexican* or *Puerto Rican*) would be more accurate. When discussing an American's heritage, often the best term to use is the country of origin plus the word *American,* as in *Swedish American* or *Mexican American.* Currently *black* and *African American* are acceptable.

Some people prefer *Native American* over *American Indian*, but both terms are used. In Canada the preferred name for indigenous peoples is *First Peoples* (or *Inuit* for those who live in the far north). *First Peoples* is increasingly used by indigenous peoples in the United States in solidarity with their Canadian relatives. If you are writing about specific people, use the name of the specific American or Canadian Indian group (*Cree, Hopi, Mi'kmaq, Ute*).

Be inclusive about people with disabilities

The *Publication Manual of the American Psychological Association* (5th ed.) offers some good advice: "Put people first, not their disability" (75). Write *people who are deaf* instead of *the deaf* and *a student who is quadriplegic* instead of *a quadriplegic student.*

Be inclusive about people of different ages

Avoid bias by choosing accurate terms to describe age. If possible, use the person's age. *Eighty-two-year-old Adele Schumacher* is better than *elderly Adele Schumacher.*

21e Recognize International Varieties of English

English today comes in various shapes and forms. Many applied linguists now speak of "World Englishes" in the plural, to highlight the diversity of the English language as it is used worldwide.

English has long been established as the dominant language in Australia, Canada, New Zealand, the United Kingdom, and the United States, although many people in those countries also use other languages at home and in their communities. Englishes used in these countries share many characteristics, but there also are some differences in sentence structures, vocabulary, spelling, and punctuation. For example:

British English The outdoor concert was **rained off.**

U.S. English The outdoor concert was **rained out**.

British English What's the price of **petrol** (petroleum) these days?

U.S. English What's the price of **gas** (gasoline) these days?

Newer varieties of English have emerged outside traditionally English-speaking countries. Many former British and U.S. colonies—Hong Kong, India, Malaysia, Nigeria, Papua New Guinea, the Philippines, Singapore, and others—continue to use a local variety of English for both public and private communication. Englishes used in many of these countries are based primarily on the British variety, but they also include many features that reflect the local context.

Indian English **Open** the air conditioner.

U.S. English **Turn on** the air conditioner.

Singaporean English I was **arrowed** to lead the discussion.

U.S. English I was **selected** to lead the discussion.

Remember that correctness differs from one variation of English to another.

Grammar

22 Fragments, Run-ons, and Comma Splices

Avoid these three common sentence errors.

 Fragments

Fragments are incomplete sentences. They are punctuated to look like sentences, but they lack a key element—often a subject or a verb—or else they are subordinate clauses or phrases. Consider this example of a full sentence followed by a fragment:

> The university's enrollment rose unexpectedly during the fall semester. **Because the percentage of students who accepted offers of admission was much higher than previous years and fewer students than usual dropped out or transferred.**

When a sentence starts with *because,* we expect to find a main clause later. Instead, the *because* clause refers back to the previous sentence. The writer no doubt knew that the fragment gave the reasons why enrollment rose, but a reader must stop to determine the connection.

In formal writing you should avoid fragments. Readers expect words punctuated as a sentence to be a complete sentence. They expect writers to complete their thoughts rather than force readers to guess the missing element.

Basic strategies for turning fragments into sentences

Incorporate the fragment into an adjoining sentence.

In many cases you can incorporate the fragment into an adjoining sentence.

> I was hooked on the ~~game. Playing~~ *game, playing* day and night.

Add the missing element.

If you cannot incorporate a fragment into another sentence, add the missing element.

> When aiming for the highest returns, ~~and~~ *investors* also ~~thinking~~ *should think* about the possible losses.

COMMON ERRORS

Recognizing fragments

If you can spot fragments, you can fix them. Grammar checkers can find some of them, but they miss many fragments and may identify other sentences wrongly as fragments. Ask these questions when you are checking for sentence fragments.

- **Does the sentence have a subject?** Except for commands, sentences need subjects:

  > Jane spent every cent of credit she had available. **And then applied for more cards.**

- **Does the sentence have a complete verb?** Sentences require complete verbs. Verbs that end in *-ing* must have an auxiliary verb to be complete.

  > Ralph keeps changing majors. **He trying to figure out what he really wants to do after college.**

- **If the sentence begins with a subordinate clause, is there a main clause in the same sentence?**

  > Even though Seattle is cloudy much of the year, no American city is more beautiful when the sun shines. **Which is one reason people continue to move there.**

Remember:

1. **A sentence must have a subject and a complete verb.**
2. **A subordinate clause cannot stand alone as a sentence.**

22b Run-on Sentences

While fragments are incomplete sentences, run-ons jam together two or more sentences, failing to separate them with appropriate punctuation.

Fixing run-on sentences

Take three steps to fix run-on sentences: (1) identify the problem, (2) determine where the run-on sentence needs to be divided, and (3) choose the punctuation that best indicates the relationship between the main clauses.

COMMON ERRORS

Recognizing run-on sentences

When you read this sentence, you realize something is wrong.

> **I do not recall what kind of printer it was all I remember is that it could sort, staple, and print a packet at the same time.**

The problem is that two main clauses are not separated by punctuation. The reader must look carefully to determine where one main clause stops and the next one begins.

> I do not recall what kind of printer it was | all I remember is that it could sort, staple, and print a packet at the same time.

A period should be placed after *was,* and the next sentence should begin with a capital letter:

> I do not recall what kind of printer it was. All I remember is that it could sort, staple, and print a packet at the same time.

Run-on sentences are major errors.

Remember: Two main clauses must be separated by correct punctuation.

1. Identify the problem.

When you read your writing aloud, run-on sentences will often trip you up, just as they confuse readers. If you find two main clauses with no punctuation separating them, you have a run-on sentence. You can also search for subject and verb pairs to check for run-ons.

> SUBJ — VERB
> **Internet businesses** are not bound to specific locations or old ways of running a business **they** are more flexible in allowing employees to telecommute and to determine the hours they work.
> (S: they; V: are)

2. Determine where the run-on sentence needs to be divided.

> Internet businesses are not bound to specific locations or old ways of running a business | they are more flexible in allowing employees to telecommute and to determine the hours they work.

3. Determine the relationship between the main clauses.

You will revise a run-on more effectively if you first determine the relationship between the main clauses and understand the effect or point you are trying to make. There are several punctuation strategies for fixing run-ons.

- **Insert a period.** This is the simplest way to fix a run-on sentence.

  > Internet businesses are not bound to specific locations or old ways of running a business. They are more flexible in allowing employees to telecommute and to determine the hours they work.

  However, if you want to indicate more clearly a closer relationship between the two main clauses, you may want to choose one of the following strategies.

- **Insert a semicolon (and possibly a transitional word specifying the relationship between the two main clauses).**

  > Internet businesses are not bound to specific locations or old ways of running a business; therefore, they are more flexible in allowing employees to telecommute and to determine the hours they work.

- **Insert a comma and a coordinating conjunction *(and, but, or, nor, for, so, yet).***

  Internet businesses are not bound to specific locations or old ways of running a business, so they are more flexible in allowing employees to telecommute and to determine the hours they work.

- **Make one of the clauses subordinate.**

  Because Internet businesses are not bound to specific locations or old ways of running a business, they are more flexible in allowing employees to telecommute and to determine the hours they work.

22c Comma Splices

Comma splices occur when two or more sentences are incorrectly joined by a comma: A comma links two clauses that could stand on their own. In this example, the comma following "classes" should be a period.

> **Most of us were taking the same classes, if someone had a question, we would all help out.**

Such sentences include a punctuation mark—a comma—separating two main clauses. However, a comma is not a strong enough punctuation mark to separate two main clauses.

Fixing comma splices

You have several options for fixing comma splices. Select the one that best fits where the sentence is located and the effect you are trying to achieve.

1. Change the comma to a period.

Most comma splices can be fixed by changing the comma to a period.

> It didn't matter that I worked in a windowless room for 40 hours a ~~week, on~~ week. On the Web I was exploring and learning more about distant people and places than I ever had before.

COMMON ERRORS

Recognizing comma splices

When you edit your writing, look carefully at sentences that contain commas. Does the sentence contain two main clauses? If so, are the main clauses joined by a comma and coordinating conjunction (*and, but, for, or, not, so, yet*)?

Incorrect The **concept** (SUBJ) of "nature" **depends** (VERB) on the concept of human "culture," the **problem** (SUBJ) **is** (V) that "culture" is itself shaped by "nature." [Two main clauses joined by only a comma]

Correct Even though the concept of "nature" depends on the concept of human "culture," "culture" is itself shaped by "nature." [Subordinate clause plus a main clause]

Correct The concept of "nature" depends on the concept of human "culture," but "culture" is itself shaped by "nature." [Two main clauses joined by a comma and coordinating conjunction]

The word *however* produces some of the most common comma splice errors. *However* usually functions to begin a main clause, and when it does it should be preceded by a semicolon rather than a comma.

Incorrect The White House press secretary repeatedly vowed the Administration was not choosing a side between the two countries embroiled in conflict, **however** the developing foreign policy suggested otherwise.

Correct The White House press secretary repeatedly vowed the Administration was not choosing a side between the two countries embroiled in conflict; **however,** the developing foreign policy suggested otherwise. [Two main clauses joined by a semicolon]

Remember: Do not use a comma as a period.

2. Change the comma to a semicolon.

A semicolon indicates a close connection between two main clauses.

> It didn't matter that I worked in a windowless room for 40 hours a ~~week,~~ week; on the Web I was exploring and learning more about distant people and places than I ever had before.

3. Insert a coordinating conjunction.

Other comma splices can be repaired by inserting a coordinating conjunction (*and, but, or, nor, so, yet, for*) to indicate the relationship of the two main clauses. The coordinating conjunction must be preceded by a comma.

> Digital technologies have intensified a global culture that affects us daily in large and small ways, **yet** their impact remains poorly understood.

4. Make one of the main clauses a subordinate clause.

If a comma splice includes one main clause that is subordinate to the other, rewrite the sentence using a subordinating conjunction.

> Because community
> ~~Community~~ is the vision of a great society trimmed down to the size of a small town, it is a powerful metaphor for real estate developers who sell a mini-utopia along with a house or condo.

5. Make one of the main clauses a phrase.

You can also rewrite one of the main clauses as a phrase.

> Community—**the vision of a great society trimmed down to the size of a small town**—is a powerful metaphor for real estate developers who sell a mini-utopia along with a house or condo.

23 Subject-Verb Agreement

Make each verb agree with its subject.

23a Agreement in the Present Tense

When your verb is in the present tense, agreement in number is straightforward: The subject takes the base form of the verb in all but the third person singular. For example, the verb *walk,* in the present tense, agrees in number with most subjects in its base form:

First person singular	I walk
Second person singular	You walk
First person plural	We walk
Second person plural	You walk
Third person plural	They walk

Third person singular subjects are the exception to this rule. When your subject is in the third person singular (*he, it, Fido, Lucy, Mr. Jones*) you need to add *s* or *es* to the base form of the verb.

Third person singular (add *s*)	He walks. It walks. Fido walks.
Third person singular (add *es*)	Lucy goes. Mr. Jones goes.

23b Singular and Plural Subjects

Follow these rules when you have trouble determining whether to use a singular or plural verb form.

Subjects joined by *and*

When two subjects are joined by *and,* treat them as a compound (plural) subject.

> **The teacher and the lawyer** are headed west to start a commune.

Some compound subjects work together as a single noun and are treated as singular. Although they appear to be compound and therefore plural, these subjects take the singular form of the verb:

> **Rock and roll** remains the devil's music, even in the twenty-first century.

When two nouns linked by *and* are modified by *every* or *each,* these two nouns are likewise treated as one singular subject:

> **Each night and day** brings no new news of you.

An exception to this rule arises when the word *each* follows a compound subject. In these cases, usage varies depending on the number of the direct object.

> **The army and the navy each** have their own air planes.
>
> **The owl and the pussycat each** has a personal claim to fame.

Subjects joined by *or, either . . . or,* or *neither . . . nor*

When a subject is joined by *or, either . . . or,* or *neither . . . nor,* make sure the verb agrees with the subject closest to the verb.

> Is it **the sky** (SING) or **the mountains** (PLURAL) that are (PL) blue?
>
> Is it **the mountains** (PLURAL) or **the sky** (SING) that surrounds (SING) us?
>
> **Neither the animals** (PLURAL) **nor the zookeeper** (SING) knows (SING) how to relock the gate.
>
> **Either a coyote** (SING) **or several dogs** (PLURAL) were (PL) howling last night.

Subjects along with another noun

Verbs agree with the subject of a sentence, even when a subject is linked to another noun with a phrase like *as well as, along with,* or *alongside.* These modifying phrases are usually set off from the main subject with commas.

IGNORE THIS PHRASE
Chicken, alongside various steamed vegetables, is my favorite meal.

IGNORE THIS PHRASE
Besides B. B. King, **John Lee Hooker and Muddy Waters** are my favorite blues artists of all time.

COMMON ERRORS

Subjects separated from verbs

The most common agreement errors occur when words come between the subject and verb. These intervening words do not affect subject-verb agreement. To ensure that you use the correct verb form, identify the subject and the verb. Ignore any phrases that come between them.

IGNORE THIS PHRASE
Incorrect **Students** at inner-city Washington High **reads** more than suburban students.

Correct **Students** at inner-city Washington High read more than suburban students.

Students is plural and *read* is plural; subject and verb agree.

Incorrect **The whale shark**, the largest of all sharks, **feed** on plankton.

Correct **The whale shark,** the largest of all sharks, feeds on plankton.

The plural noun *sharks* that appears between the subject *the whale shark* and the verb *feeds* does not change the number of the subject. The subject is singular and the verb is singular. Subject and verb agree.

Remember: When you check for subject-verb agreement, identify the subject and the verb. Ignore any words that come between them.

23c Indefinite Pronouns as Subjects

The choice of a singular or plural pronoun is determined by the **antecedent**—the noun that pronoun refers to. Indefinite pronouns, such as *some, few, all, someone, everyone,* and *each,* often do not refer to identifiable subjects; hence they have no antecedents. Most indefinite pronouns are singular and agree with the singular forms of verbs. Some, like *both* and *many,* are always plural and agree with the plural forms of verbs. Other indefinite pronouns are variable and can agree with either singular or plural verb forms, depending on the context of the sentence.

COMMON ERRORS

Agreement errors using *each*

When a pronoun is singular, its verb must be singular. A common stumbling block to this rule is the pronoun *each. Each* is always treated as a singular pronoun in college writing. When *each* stands alone, the choice is easy to make:

Incorrect Each **are** an outstanding student.

Correct Each **is** an outstanding student.

But when *each* is modified by a phrase that includes a plural noun, the choice of a singular verb form becomes less obvious:

Incorrect Each of the girls **are** fit.

Correct Each of the girls **is** fit.

Incorrect Each of our dogs **get** a present.

Correct Each of our dogs **gets** a present.

Remember: *Each* is always singular.

23d Collective Nouns as Subjects

Collective nouns refer to groups (*audience, class, committee, crowd, family, government, group, jury, public, team*). When members of a group are considered as a unit, use singular verbs and singular pronouns.

> The **crowd** is unusually quiet at the moment, but it will get noisy soon.

When members of a group are considered as individuals, use plural verbs and plural pronouns.

> The **faculty** have their differing opinions on how to address the problems caused by reduced state support.

Sometimes collective nouns can be singular in one context and plural in another. Writers must decide which verb form to use based on sentence context.

> The **number** of people who live downtown is increasing.

> A **number** of people are moving downtown from the suburbs.

23e Inverted Word Order

In English a sentence's subject usually comes before the verb: *The nights are tender*. Sometimes, however, you will come across a sentence with inverted word order: *Tender are the nights*. Here the subject of the sentence, *nights*, comes after the verb, *are*. Writers use inverted word order most often in forming questions. The statement *Cats are friendly* becomes a question when you invert the subject and the verb: *Are cats friendly?* Writers also use inverted word order for added emphasis or for style considerations.

Do not be confused by inverted word order. Locate the subject of your sentence, then make sure your verb agrees with that subject.

23f Amounts, Numbers, and Pairs

Subjects that describe amounts of money, time, distance, or measurement are singular and require singular verbs.

Three days is never long enough to unwind.

Some subjects, such as courses of study, academic specializations, illnesses, and even some nations, are treated as singular subjects even though their names end in *-s* or *-es*. For example, *economics, news, ethics, measles*, and *the United States* all end in *-s* but are all singular subjects.

Economics is a rich field of study.

Other subjects require a plural verb form even though they refer to single items such as *jeans, slacks, glasses, scissors,* and *tweezers*. These items are all pairs.

My **glasses** are scratched.

24 Verbs

Spot and fix problems with verbs.

24a Basic Verb Forms

Almost all verbs in English have five possible forms. The exception is the verb *be*. Regular verbs follow this basic pattern:

Base form	Third-person singular	Past tense	Past participle	Present participle
jump	jumps	jumped	jumped	jumping
like	likes	liked	liked	liking
talk	talks	talked	talked	talking
wish	wishes	wished	wished	wishing

Base form

The base form of the verb is the one you find listed in the dictionary. This form indicates an action or condition in the present.

I like New York in June.

Third person singular

Third person singular subjects include *he, she, it,* and the nouns they replace, as well as other pronouns, including *someone, anybody,* and *everything.* Present tense verbs in the third person singular end with *s* or *es.*

Ms. Nessan speaks in riddles.

Past tense

The past tense describes an action or condition that occurred in the past. For most verbs, the past tense is formed by adding *d* or *ed* to the base form of the verb.

She inhaled the night air.

Many verbs, however, have irregular past tense forms. (See Section 24b.)

Past participle

The past participle is used with *have* to form verbs in the perfect tense, with *be* to form verbs in the passive voice (see Section 18a), and to form adjectives derived from verbs.

Past perfect	They **had** gone to the grocery store prematurely.
Passive	The book **was** written thirty years before it was published.
Adjective	In the eighties, teased hair was all the rage.

COMMON ERRORS

Missing verb endings

Verb endings are not always pronounced in speech, especially in some dialects of English. It's also easy to omit these endings when you are writing quickly. Spelling checkers will not mark these errors, so you have to find them while proofreading.

Incorrect Jeremy **feel** as if he's catching a cold.

Correct Jeremy **feels** as if he's catching a cold.

Incorrect Sheila **hope** she would get the day off.

Correct Sheila **hoped** she would get the day off.

Remember: Check verbs carefully for missing *s* or *es* endings in the present tense and missing *d* or *ed* endings in the past tense.

Present participle

The present participle functions in one of three ways. Used with an auxiliary verb, it can describe a continuing action. The present participle can also function as a noun, known as a **gerund**, or as an adjective. The present participle is formed by adding *ing* to the base form of a verb.

Present participle	Wild elks **are** **competing** for limited food resources.
Gerund	**Sailing** around the Cape of Good Hope is rumored to bring good luck.
Adjective	We looked for shells in the **ebbing** tide.

24b Irregular Verbs

A verb is **regular** when its past and past participle forms are created by adding *ed* or *d* to the base form. If this rule does not apply, the verb is considered an **irregular** verb. Here are selected common irregular verbs and their basic conjugations.

Common irregular verbs

Base form	Past tense	Past participle
be (is, am, are)	was, were	been
become	became	become
bring	brought	brought
come	came	come
do	did	done
get	got	got or gotten
have	had	had
go	went	gone
know	knew	known
see	saw	seen

COMMON ERRORS

Past tense forms of irregular verbs

The past tense and past participle forms of irregular verbs are often confused. The most frequent error is using a past tense form instead of the past participle with *had*.

Incorrect She had never **rode** (PAST TENSE) a horse before.

Correct She had never **ridden** (PAST PARTICIPLE) a horse before.

COMMON ERRORS (continued)

Incorrect	He had saw many alligators in Louisiana. (PAST TENSE: saw)
Correct	He had seen many alligators in Louisiana. (PAST PARTICIPLE: seen)

Remember: Change any past tense verbs preceded by *had* to past participles.

24c Transitive and Intransitive Verbs

Lay/lie, set/sit, and *raise/rise*

Do your house keys lay or lie on the kitchen table? Does a book set or sit on the shelf? *Raise/rise, lay/lie,* and *set/sit* are transitive/intransitive verb pairs that writers frequently confuse. Transitive verbs take direct objects—nouns that receive the action of the verb. Intransitive verbs act in sentences that lack direct objects.

Transitive Henry sets the book [direct object, the book being set] on the shelf.

Intransitive Henry sits down to read the book.

The following charts list the trickiest pairs of transitive and intransitive verbs and the correct forms for each verb tense. Pay special attention to *lay* and *lie,* which are irregular.

	lay (put something down)	**lie (recline)**
Present	lay, lays	lie, lies
Present participle	laying	lying
Past	laid	lay
Past participle	laid	lain

Transitive When you complete your test, please lay your pencil [direct object, the thing being laid down] on the desk.

Intransitive The *Titanic* lies upright in two pieces at a depth of 13,000 feet.

	raise (elevate something)	**rise (get up)**
Present	raise, raises	rise, rises
Present participle	raising	rising
Past	raised	rose
Past participle	raised	risen

Transitive We raise our glasses [direct object, the things being raised] to toast Uncle Han.

Intransitive The sun rises over the bay.

	set (place something)	**sit (take a seat)**
Present	set, sets	sit, sits
Present participle	setting	sitting
Past	set	sat
Past participle	set	sat

Transitive Every morning Stanley sets two dollars [direct object, the things being set] on the table to tip the waiter.

Intransitive I sit in the front seat if it's available.

25 Pronouns

Recognize misused pronouns and correct them.

25a Pronoun Case

Subjective pronouns function as the subjects of sentences. **Objective pronouns** function as direct or indirect objects. **Possessive pronouns** indicate ownership.

Subjective pronouns	Objective pronouns	Possessive pronouns
I	me	my, mine
we	us	our, ours
you	you	your, yours
he	him	his
she	her	her, hers
it	it	its
they	them	their, theirs
who	whom	whose

Pronouns in compound phrases

Picking the right pronoun can sometimes be confusing when the pronoun appears in a compound phrase.

> If we work together, you and **me** can get the job done quickly.
>
> If we work together, you and **I** can get the job done quickly.

Which is correct—*me* or *I*? Removing the other pronoun usually makes the choice clear.

Incorrect Me can get the job done quickly.

Correct I can get the job done quickly.

We and *us* before nouns

Another pair of pronouns that can cause difficulty is *we* and *us* before nouns.

Us friends must stick together.

We friends must stick together.

Which is correct—*us* or *we*? Removing the noun indicates the correct choice.

Incorrect Us must stick together.

Correct We must stick together.

Who versus *whom*

Choosing between *who* and *whom* is often difficult, even for experienced writers. The distinction between *who* and *whom* is disappearing from spoken language. *Who* is more often used in spoken language, even when *whom* is correct.

COMMON ERRORS

Who or *Whom*

In writing, the distinction between *who* and *whom* is still often observed. *Who* and *whom* follow the same rules as other pronouns: *Who* is the subject pronoun; *whom* is the object pronoun. If you are dealing with an object, *whom* is the correct choice.

Incorrect Who did you send the letter to?
Who did you give the present to?

COMMON ERRORS (continued)

Correct To whom did you send the letter?
Whom did you give the present to?

Who is always the right choice for the subject pronoun.

Correct Who gave you the present?
Who brought the cookies?

If you are uncertain of which one to use, try substituting *she* and *her* or *he* and *him*.

Incorrect You sent the letter to **she** **[who]**?

Correct You sent the letter to her **[whom]**?

Incorrect **Him** **[Whom]** gave you the present?

Correct He **[Who]** gave you the present?

Remember: ***Who*** **= subject**
Whom **= object**

Whoever versus *whomever*

With the rule regarding *who* and *whom* in mind, you can distinguish between *whoever* and *whomever*. Which is correct?

Her warmth touched **whoever** she met.

Her warmth touched **whomever** she met.

In this sentence the pronoun functions as the direct object in its own clause: she met whomever. Thus *whomever* is the correct choice.

Pronouns in comparisons

When you write a sentence using a comparison that includes *than* or *as* followed by a pronoun, usually you will have to think about which pronoun is correct. Which of the following is correct?

Vimala is a faster swimmer than **him**.

Vimala is a faster swimmer than **he**.

The test that will give you the correct answer is to add the verb that finishes the sentence—in this case, *is*.

Incorrect Vimala is a faster swimmer than **him is.**

Correct Vimala is a faster swimmer than **he is.**

Adding the verb makes the correct choice evident.

Possessive pronouns

Possessive pronouns are confusing at times because possessive nouns are formed with apostrophes, but possessive pronouns do not require apostrophes. Pronouns that use apostrophes are always **contractions**.

It's = It is
Who's = Who is
They're = They are

The test for whether to use an apostrophe is to determine whether the pronoun is possessive or a contraction. The most confusing pair is *its* and *it's*.

Incorrect **Its** a sure thing she will be elected. [Contraction needed]

Correct **It's** a sure thing she will be elected. [**It is** a sure thing.]

Incorrect The dog lost **it's** collar. [Possessive needed]

Correct The dog lost **its** collar.

Possessive pronouns before *-ing* verbs

Pronouns that modify an *-ing* verb (called a *gerund*) or an *-ing* verb phrase (*gerund phrase*) should appear in the possessive.

Incorrect The odds of **you** making the team are excellent.

Correct The odds of **your** making the team are excellent.

25b Pronoun Agreement

Because pronouns usually replace or refer to other nouns, they must match those nouns in number and gender. The noun that the pronoun replaces is called its **antecedent**. If pronoun and antecedent match, they are in **agreement**. When a pronoun is close to the antecedent, usually there is no problem.

> **Maria** forgot her coat.
>
> The band **members** collected their uniforms.

Pronoun agreement errors often happen when pronouns and the nouns they replace are separated by several words.

Incorrect

> The **players**, exhausted from the double-overtime game, picked up **his** sweats and walked toward the locker rooms.

Correct

> The **players**, exhausted from the double-overtime game, picked up their sweats and walked toward the locker rooms.

Careful writers make sure that pronouns match their antecedents.

Collective nouns

Collective nouns (such as *audience, class, committee, crowd, family, herd, jury, team*) can be singular or plural depending on whether the emphasis is on the group or on its individual members.

Correct The **committee** was unanimous in its decision.

Correct The **committee** put their opinions ahead of the goals of the unit.

COMMON ERRORS

Indefinite pronouns

Indefinite pronouns (such as *anybody, anything, each, either, everybody, everything, neither, none, somebody, something*) refer to unspecified people or things. Most take singular pronouns.

Incorrect Everybody can choose **their** roommates.

Correct Everybody can choose **his or her** roommate.

Correct alternative All students can choose **their** roommates.

A few indefinite pronouns (*all, any, either, more, most, neither, none, some*) can take either singular or plural pronouns.

Correct **Some** of the shipment was damaged when **it** became overheated.

Correct **All** thought **they** should have a good seat at the concert.

A few pronouns are always plural (*few, many, several*).

Correct **Several** want refunds.

Remember: Words that begin with *any, some,* and *every* are usually singular.

COMMON ERRORS

Pronoun agreement with compound antecedents

Antecedents joined by *and* take plural pronouns.

Correct *Moncef and Driss* practiced **their** music.

Exception: When compound antecedents are preceded by *each* or *every,* use a singular pronoun.

Correct **Every male cardinal and warbler** arrives before the female to define **its** territory.

When compound antecedents are connected by *or* or *nor,* the pronoun agrees with the antecedent closer to it.

Incorrect **Either the Ross twins or Angela** should bring **their** CDs.

Correct **Either the Ross twins or Angela** should bring **her** CDs.

Better **Either Angela or the Ross twins** should bring **their** CDs.

When you put the plural *twins* last, the correct choice becomes the plural pronoun *their.*

Remember:

1. **Use plural pronouns for antecedents joined by *and.***
2. **Use singular pronouns for antecedents preceded by *each* or *every.***
3. **Use a pronoun that agrees with the nearest antecedent when compound antecedents are joined by *or* or *nor.***

25c Avoid Sexist Pronouns

English does not have a neutral singular pronoun for a group of mixed genders or a person of unknown gender. Referring to a group of mixed genders using male pronouns is unacceptable to many people. Unless the school in the following example is all male, many readers would object to the use of *his*.

Sexist **Each student** must select **his** courses using the online registration system.

One strategy is to use *her or his* or *his or her* instead of *his*.

Correct **Each student** must select **his or her** courses using the online registration system.

Often you can avoid using *his or her* by changing the noun to the plural form.

Better **All students** must select **their** courses using the online registration system.

In some cases, however, using *his or her* is necessary.

25d Vague Reference

Pronouns can sometimes refer to more than one noun, thus confusing readers.

> The **coach** rushed past the injured **player** to yell at the **referee**. **She** was hit in the face by a stray elbow.

You have to guess which person *she* refers to—the coach, the player, or the referee. Sometimes you cannot even guess the antecedent of a pronoun.

> The new subdivision destroyed the last remaining habitat for wildlife within the city limits. **They** have ruined our city with their unchecked greed.

Whom does *they* refer to? the mayor and city council? the developers? the people who live in the subdivision? or all of the above?

Pronouns should never leave the reader guessing about antecedents. If different nouns can be confused as the antecedent, then the ambiguity should be clarified.

Vague Mafalda's pet boa constrictor crawled across Tonya's foot. **She** was mortified.

Better When Mafalda's pet boa constrictor crawled across Tonya's foot, **Mafalda** was mortified.

COMMON ERRORS

Vague use of *this*

Always use a noun immediately after *this, that, these, those,* and *some.*

Vague Enrique asked Meg to remove the viruses on his computer. **This** was a bad idea.

Was it a bad idea for Enrique to ask Meg because she was insulted? Because she didn't know how? Because removing viruses would destroy some of Enrique's files?

Better Enrique asked Meg to remove the viruses on his computer. **This imposition** on Meg's time was a bad idea.

Remember: Ask yourself "this *what?*" and add the noun that *this* refers to.

26 Shifts

Watch for unintentional shifts in tense, mood, voice, or number.

26a Shifts in Tense

Appropriate shifts in verb tense

Changes in verb tense are sometimes necessary to indicate a shift in time.

Past to future Because Oda won [PAST TENSE] the lottery, she will quit [FUTURE TENSE] her job at the hospital as soon as her supervisor finds a [PRESENT TENSE] qualified replacement.

Inappropriate shifts in verb tense

Be careful to avoid confusing your reader with shifts in verb tense.

Incorrect While Brazil looks [PRESENT TENSE] to ecotourism to fund rain forest preservation, other South American nations relied [PAST TENSE] on foreign aid and conservation efforts.

The shift from present tense (*looks*) to past tense (*relied*) is confusing. Correct the mistake by putting both verbs in the present tense.

Correct While Brazil looks [PRESENT TENSE] to ecotourism to fund rain forest preservation, other South American nations rely [PRESENT TENSE] on foreign aid and conservation efforts.

COMMON ERRORS

Unnecessary tense shift

Notice the tense shift in the following example.

Incorrect

PAST TENSE
In May of 2000 the "I Love You" virus crippled the computer
PAST TENSE
systems of major American companies and irritated millions of
PRESENT TENSE
private computer users. As the virus generates millions of
PRESENT TENSE
e-mails and erases millions of computer files, companies such
PRESENT TENSE
as Ford and Time Warner are forced to shut down their clogged
e-mail systems.

The second sentence shifts unnecessarily to the present tense, confusing the reader. Did the "I Love You" virus have its heyday several years ago, or is it still wreaking havoc now? Changing the verbs in the second sentence to the past tense eliminates the confusion.

Correct

PAST TENSE
In May of 2000 the "I Love You" virus crippled the computer
PAST TENSE
systems of major American companies and irritated millions of
PAST TENSE
private computer users. As the virus generated millions of
PAST TENSE
e-mails and erased millions of computer files, companies such
PAST TENSE
as Ford and Time Warner were forced to shut down their clogged
e-mail systems.

Remember: Shift verb tense only when you are referring to different time periods.

26b Shifts in Mood

Verbs can be categorized into three moods—indicative, imperative, and subjunctive—defined by the functions they serve.

Indicative verbs state facts, opinions, and questions.

Fact NASA plans to return the Space Shuttle to flight this year.

Imperative verbs make commands, give advice, and make requests.

Command Investigate the cause of the accident so the Shuttle can return to flight.

Subjunctive verbs express wishes, unlikely or untrue situations, hypothetical situations, requests with *that* clauses, and suggestions.

Unlikely or untrue situation If fixing the Shuttle were as simple as the news media made it out to be, NASA would be flying missions by now.

Be careful not to shift from one mood to another in mid-sentence.

Incorrect If the government **were** to shift funding priorities away from the Shuttle, NASA scientists **lose** even more time in getting the Shuttle flying again.

The sudden shift from subjunctive to indicative mood in this sentence is confusing. Are the scientists losing time now, or is losing time a likely result of a government funding shift? Revise the sentence to keep both verbs in the subjunctive.

Correct If the government **were** to shift funding priorities away from the Shuttle, NASA scientists would lose even more time in getting the Shuttle flying again.

26c Shifts in Voice

Watch for unintended shifts from active (*I ate the cookies*) to passive voice (*the cookies were eaten*).

Incorrect The sudden storm toppled several trees and numerous windows **were shattered.**

The unexpected shift from active voice (*toppled*) to passive (*were broken*) forces readers to wonder whether it was the sudden storm, or something else, that broke the windows.

Correct The sudden storm toppled several trees and shattered numerous windows.

Revising the sentence to eliminate the shift to passive voice (see Section 18a) also improves its parallel structure (see 20c).

26d Shifts in Person and Number

Sudden shifts from third person (*he, she, it, one*) to first (*I, we*) or second (*you*) are confusing to readers and often indicate a writer's uncertainty about how to address a reader. We often make such shifts in spoken English, but in formal writing shifts in person need to be recognized and corrected.

Incorrect When **one** is reading a magazine, **you** often see several different type fonts used on a single page.

The shift from third person to second person in this sentence is confusing.

Correct When reading a magazine you often see several different type fonts used on a single page.

Similarly, shifts from singular to plural subjects (see Section 23b) within a single sentence also confuse readers.

Incorrect Administrators often make more money than professors, but only **a professor** has frequent contact with students.

Correct Administrators often make more money than professors, but only professors have frequent contact with students.

The revised sentence eliminates a distracting and unnecessary shift from plural to singular.

27 Modifiers

Give life to your writing with modifiers.

27a Choose the Correct Modifier

Modifiers come in two varieties: adjectives and adverbs. The same words can function as adjectives or adverbs, depending on what they modify.

Adjectives modify

nouns—*iced* tea, *power* forward
pronouns—He is *brash*.

Adverbs modify

verbs—*barely* reach, drive *carefully*
adjectives—*truly* brave activist, *shockingly* red lipstick
other adverbs—*not* soon forget, *very* well
clauses—*Honestly,* I find ballet boring.

Adjectives answer the questions *Which one? How many?* and *What kind?* Adverbs answer the questions *How often? To what extent? When? Where? How?* and *Why?*

Use the correct forms of comparatives and superlatives

Comparative modifiers weigh one thing against another. They either end in *er* or are preceded by *more.*

Road bikes are faster on pavement than mountain bikes.

The more courageous juggler tossed flaming torches.

Superlative modifiers compare three or more items. They either end in *est* or are preceded by *most.*

April is the **hottest** month in New Delhi.

Wounded animals are the **most ferocious**.

Some frequently used comparatives and superlatives are irregular. The following list can help you become familiar with them.

Adjective	**Comparative**	**Superlative**
good	better	best
bad	worse	worst
little (amount)	less	least
many, much	more	most
Adverb	**Comparative**	**Superlative**
well	better	best
badly	worse	worst

Do not use both a suffix (*er* or *est*) and *more* or *most*.

Incorrect The service at Jane's Restaurant is **more slower** than the service at Alphonso's.

Correct The service at Jane's Restaurant is **slower** than the service at Alphonso's.

Absolute modifiers are words that represent an unvarying condition and thus aren't subject to the degrees that comparative and superlative constructions convey. Common absolute modifiers include *complete, ultimate,* and *unique. Unique,* for example, means "one of a kind." There's nothing else like it. Thus something cannot be *very unique* or *totally unique*. It is either unique or it isn't. Absolute modifiers should not be modified by comparatives (*more* + modifier or modifier + *er*) or superlatives (*most* + modifier or modifier + *est*).

Double negatives

In English, as in mathematics, two negatives equal a positive. Avoid using two negative words in one sentence, or you'll end up saying the opposite of what you mean. The following are negative words that you should avoid doubling up:

barely	nobody	nothing
hardly	none	scarcely
neither	no one	

Incorrect, double negative **Barely no one** noticed that the pop star lip-synched during the whole performance.

Correct, single negative **Barely anyone** noticed that the pop star lip-synched during the whole performance.

Incorrect, double negative When the pastor asked if anyone had objections to the marriage, **nobody** said **nothing.**

Correct, single negative When the pastor asked if anyone had objections to the marriage, **nobody** said **anything**.

27b Place Adjectives Carefully

As a general rule, the closer you place a modifier to the word it modifies, the less the chance you will confuse your reader.

Confusing **Watching from the ground below**, the kettle of broadwing hawks circled high above the observers.

Is the kettle of hawks watching from the ground below? You can fix the problem by putting the modified subject immediately after the modifier or placing the modifier next to the modified subject.

Better The kettle of broadwing hawks circled high above the **observers** **who were watching from the ground below**.

Better **Watching from the ground below,** the **observers** saw a kettle of broadwing hawks circle high above them.

27c Place Adverbs Carefully

Single-word adverbs and adverbial clauses and phrases can usually sit comfortably either before or after the words they modify.

> Dimitri quietly **walked** down the hall.
>
> Dimitri **walked** quietly down the hall.

Conjunctive adverbs—*also, however, instead, likewise, then, therefore, thus,* and others—are adverbs that show how ideas relate to one another. They prepare a reader for contrasts, exceptions, additions, conclusions, and other shifts in an argument. Conjunctive adverbs can usually fit well into more than one place in the sentence. In the following example, *however* could fit in three different places.

Between two main clauses

> Professional football players earn exorbitant salaries; however, they pay for their wealth with lifetimes of chronic pain and debilitating injuries.

Within second main clause

> Professional football players earn exorbitant salaries; they pay for their wealth, however, with lifetimes of chronic pain and debilitating injuries.

At end of second main clause

> Professional football players earn exorbitant salaries; they pay for their wealth with lifetimes of chronic pain and debilitating injuries however.

Subordinating conjunctions—words such as *after, although, because, if, since, than, that, though, when,* and *where*—often begin **adverb clauses**. Notice that we can place adverb clauses with subordinating conjunctions either before or after the word(s) being modified:

> After someone in the audience yelled, he **forgot** the lyrics.
>
> He **forgot** the lyrics after someone in the audience yelled.

COMMON ERRORS

Placement of limiting modifiers

Words such as *almost, even, hardly, just, merely, nearly, not, only,* and *simply* are called limiting modifiers. Although people often play fast and loose with their placement in everyday speech, limiting modifiers should always go immediately before the word or words they modify in your writing. Like other limiting modifiers, *only* should be placed immediately before the word it modifies.

Incorrect The Gross Domestic Product **only** gives one indicator of economic growth.

Correct The Gross Domestic Product gives **only** one indicator of economic growth.

The word *only* modifies *one* in this sentence, not *Gross Domestic Product.*

Remember: Place limiting modifiers immediately before the word(s) they modify.

27d Hyphens with Compound Modifiers

When to hyphenate

Hyphenate a compound modifier that precedes a noun.

When a compound modifier precedes a noun, you should usually hyphenate the modifier. A **compound modifier** consists of words that join together as a unit to modify a noun.

middle-class values self-fulfilling prophecy

Hyphenate a phrase when it is used as a modifier that precedes a noun.

all-you-can-eat buffet step-by-step instructions

Hyphenate the prefixes *pro-*, *anti-*, *post-*, *pre-*, *neo-*, and *mid-* before proper nouns.

neo-Nazi racism mid-Atlantic states

Hyphenate a compound modifier with a number when it precedes a noun.

eighteenth-century drama one-way street

When not to hyphenate

Do not hyphenate a compound modifier that follows a noun.

The instructor's approach is student centered.

Do not hyphenate compound modifiers when the first word is *very* or ends in *ly*.

newly recorded data very cold day

27e Revise Dangling Modifiers

Some modifiers are ambiguous because they could apply to more than one word or clause. Dangling modifiers are ambiguous for the opposite reason; they don't have a word to modify. In such cases the modifier is usually an introductory clause or phrase. What is being modified should immediately follow the phrase, but in the following sentence it is absent.

> **After bowling a perfect game,** Surfside Lanes hung Marco's photo on the wall.

You can eliminate a dangling modifier in two ways:

1. Insert the noun or pronoun being modified immediately after the introductory modifying phrase.

   After bowling a perfect game, **Marco** was honored by having his photo hung on the wall at Surfside Lanes.

2. Rewrite the introductory phrase as an introductory clause to include the noun or pronoun.

   After **Marco** bowled a perfect game, Surfside Lanes hung his photo on the wall.

COMMON ERRORS

Dangling modifiers

A dangling modifier does not seem to modify anything in a sentence; it dangles, unconnected to the word or words it presumably is intended to modify. Frequently, it produces funny results:

> **When still a girl,** my father joined the army.

It sounds like *father* was once a girl. The problem is that the subject, *I,* is missing:

> **When I was still a girl,** my father joined the army.

Remember: Modifiers should be clearly connected to the words they modify, especially at the beginning of sentences.

28 Grammar for Multilingual Writers

You can overcome the challenges of writing in a second language.

28a Nouns

Perhaps the most troublesome conventions for nonnative speakers are those that guide usage of the common articles *the, a,* and *an*. To understand how articles work in English, you must first understand how the language uses **nouns**.

Kinds of nouns

There are two basic kinds of nouns. A **proper noun** begins with a capital letter and names a unique person, place, or thing: *George W. Bush, Russia, Eiffel Tower.*

The other basic kind of noun is called a **common noun**. Common nouns do not name a unique person, place, or thing: *man, country, tower.*

Count and noncount nouns

Common nouns can be classified as either *count* or *noncount*. **Count nouns** can be made plural, usually by adding *-s* (*finger, fingers*) or by using their plural forms (*person, people; datum, data*). **Noncount nouns** cannot be counted directly and cannot take the plural form (*information,* but not *informations; garbage,* but not *garbages*). Some nouns can be either count or noncount, depending on how they are used. *Hair* can refer to either a strand of hair, where it serves as a count noun, or a mass of hair, where it becomes a noncount noun.

COMMON ESL ERRORS

Singular and plural forms of count nouns

Count nouns are simpler to quantify than noncount nouns. But remember that English requires you to state both singular and plural forms of nouns explicitly. Look at the following sentences.

Incorrect The three **bicyclist** shaved their **leg** before the big race.

Correct The three **bicyclists** shaved their **legs** before the big race.

Remember: English requires you to use plural forms of count nouns even if a plural number is otherwise indicated.

 Articles

Articles indicate that a noun is about to appear, and they clarify what the noun refers to. There are only two kinds of articles in English, definite and indefinite:

1. **the:** *The* is a **definite article**, meaning that it refers to (1) a specific object already known to the reader, (2) one about to be made known to the reader, or (3) a unique object.
2. **a, an:** The **indefinite articles** *a* and *an* refer to an object whose specific identity is not known to the reader. The only difference between *a* and *an* is that *a* is used before a consonant sound (*man, friend, yellow*), while *an* is used before a vowel sound (*animal, enemy, orange*).

COMMON ESL ERRORS

Articles with count and noncount nouns

Knowing how to distinguish between count and noncount nouns can help you decide which article to use. Noncount nouns are never used with the indefinite articles *a* or *an*.

Incorrect Maria jumped into **a** water.

Correct Maria jumped into **the** water.

No articles are used with noncount and plural count nouns when you wish to state something that has a general application.

Incorrect **The** water is a precious natural resource.

Correct Water is a precious natural resource.

Remember:

1. **Noncount nouns are never used with *a* and *an*.**
2. **Noncount and plural nouns used to make general statements do not take articles.**

28c Verbs

The verb system in English can be divided between simple verbs like *run, speak,* and *look,* and verb phrases like *may have run, have spoken,* and *will be looking*. In these examples, the words that appear before the main verbs—*may, have, will,* and *be*—are called **auxiliary verbs** (also called **helping verbs**).

Indicating tense and voice with *be* verbs

Like the other auxiliary verbs *have* and *do, be* changes form to signal tense. In addition to *be* itself, the **be verbs** are *is, am, are, was, were,* and *been.* To show ongoing action, *be* verbs are followed by the present participle, which is a verb with an *-ing* ending:

Incorrect I **am think** of all the things I'd rather **be do**.

Correct I **am thinking** of all the things I'd rather **be doing**.

To show that an action is being done to, rather than by, the subject, follow *be* verbs with the past participle (a verb usually ending in *-ed, -en,* or *-t*):

Incorrect The movie **was direct** by John Woo.

Correct The movie **was directed** by John Woo.

Modal auxiliary verbs

Modal auxiliary verbs *will, would, can, could, may, might, shall, must,* and *should* express conditions like possibility, permission, speculation, expectation, obligation, and necessity. Unlike the auxiliary verbs *be, have,* and *do,* modal verbs do not change form based on the grammatical subject of the sentence (*I, you, she, he, it, we, they*).

Two basic rules apply to all uses of modal verbs. First, modal verbs are always followed by the simple form of the verb. The simple form is the verb by itself, in the present tense, such as *have* but not *had, having,* or *to have.*

Incorrect She should **studies** harder to pass the exam.

Correct She should **study** harder to pass the exam.

The second rule is that you should not use modals consecutively.

Incorrect If you work harder at writing, you **might could** improve.

Correct If you work harder at writing, you **might** improve.

PART 6

Punctuation and Mechanics

29 Commas

Commas provide readers with vital clues for reading a sentence.

29a Commas with Introductory Elements

Introductory elements usually need to be set off by commas. Introductory words or phrases signal a shift in ideas or a particular arrangement of ideas; they help direct the reader's attention to the writer's most important points.

When a conjunctive adverb or introductory phrase begins a sentence, the comma follows.

> **Therefore**, the suspect could not have been at the scene of the crime.
>
> **Above all**, remember to let water drip from the faucets if the temperature drops below freezing.

When a conjunctive adverb comes in the middle of a sentence, set it off with commas preceding and following.

> If you really want to prevent your pipes from freezing, **however**, you should insulate them before the winter comes.

Occasionally the conjunctive adverb or phrase blends into a sentence so smoothly that a pause would sound awkward.

Awkward Even if you take every precaution, the pipes in your home may freeze, **nevertheless**.

Better Even if you take every precaution, the pipes in your home may freeze **nevertheless**.

COMMON ERRORS

Commas with long introductory modifiers

Long subordinate clauses or phrases that begin sentences should be followed by a comma. The following sentence lacks the needed comma.

Incorrect Because cell phones now have organizers and email stand-alone personal digital assistants have become another technology of the past.

When you read this sentence, you likely had to go back to sort it out. The words *organizers and email stand-alone personal digital assistants* tend to run together. When the comma is added, the sentence is easier to understand because the reader knows where the subordinate clause ends and where the main clause begins:

Correct Because cell phones now have organizers and email, stand-alone personal digital assistants have become another technology of the past.

How long is a long introductory modifier? Short introductory adverbial phrases and clauses of five words or fewer can get by without the comma if the omission does not mislead the reader. Using the comma is still correct after short introductory adverbial phrases and clauses:

Correct In the long run stocks have always done better than bonds.

Correct In the long run, stocks have always done better than bonds.

Remember: Put commas after long introductory modifiers.

29b Commas with Compound Clauses

Two main clauses joined by a coordinating conjunction (*and, or, so, yet, but, nor, for*) form a compound sentence. Writers sometimes get confused about when to insert a comma before a coordinating conjunction.

Use a comma and a coordinating conjunction to separate main clauses

Main clauses carry enough grammatical weight to be punctuated as sentences. When two main clauses are joined by a coordinating conjunction, place a comma before the coordinating conjunction in order to distinguish them.

> Sandy borrowed two boxes full of DVDs on Tuesday, **and** she returned them on Friday.

Very short main clauses joined by a coordinating conjunction do not need commas.

> She called **and** she called, but no one answered.

Do not use a comma to separate two verbs with the same subject

Incorrect Sandy borrowed two boxes full of DVDs on Tuesday, and returned them on Friday.

Sandy is the subject of both *borrowed* and *returned.* This sentence has only one main clause; it should not be punctuated as a compound sentence.

Correct Sandy borrowed two boxes full of DVDs on Tuesday and returned them on Friday.

Do not use a comma to separate a main clause from a restrictive clause or phrase

When clauses and phrases that follow the main clause are essential to the meaning of a sentence, they should not be set off with a comma.

Incorrect Sandy plans to borrow Felicia's DVD collection, while Felicia is on vacation.

Correct Sandy plans to borrow Felicia's DVD collection while Felicia is on vacation.

COMMON ERRORS

Commas in compound sentences

The easiest way to distinguish between compound sentences and sentences with phrases that follow the main clause is to isolate the part that comes after the conjunction. If the part that follows the conjunction can stand on its own as a complete sentence, insert a comma. If it cannot, omit the comma.

Main clause plus phrases

Mario thinks he lost his passport while riding the bus or by absentmindedly leaving it on the counter when he checked into the hostel.

Look at what comes after the coordinating conjunction *or:*

by absentmindedly leaving it on the counter when he checked into the hostel

This group of words is not a main clause and cannot stand on its own as a complete sentence. Do not set it off with a comma.

Main clauses joined with a conjunction

On Saturday Mario went to the American consulate to get a new passport, but the officer told him that replacement passports could not be issued on weekends.

Read the clause after the coordinating conjunction *but:*

the officer told him that replacement passports could not be issued on weekends

This group of words can stand on its own as a complete sentence. Thus, it is a main clause; place a comma before *but.*

COMMON ERRORS (continued)

Remember:
1. **Place a comma before the coordinating conjunction (*and, but, for, or, nor, so, yet*) when there are two main clauses.**
2. **Do not use a comma before the coordinating conjunction when there is only one main clause.**

COMMON ERRORS

Do not use a comma to set off a *because* clause that follows a main clause

Writers frequently place unnecessary commas before *because* and similar subordinate conjunctions that follow a main clause. *Because* is not a coordinating conjunction; thus it should not be set off by a comma unless the comma improves readability.

Incorrect I struggled to complete my term papers last year, because I didn't know how to type.

Correct I struggled to complete my term papers last year because I didn't know how to type.

But do use a comma after an introductory *because* clause.

Incorrect Because Danny left his red jersey at home Coach Russell benched him.

Correct Because Danny left his red jersey at home, Coach Russell benched him.

Remember: Use a comma after a *because* clause that begins a sentence. Do not use a comma to set off a *because* clause that follows a main clause.

29c Commas with Nonrestrictive Modifiers

Imagine that you are sending a friend a group photo that includes your aunt. Which sentence is correct?

> In the back row the woman wearing the pink hat is my aunt.

> In the back row the woman, wearing the pink hat, is my aunt.

Both sentences can be correct depending on what is in the photo. If there are three women standing in the back row and only one is wearing a pink hat, this piece of information is necessary for identifying your aunt. In this case the sentence without commas is correct because it identifies your aunt as the woman wearing the pink hat. Such necessary modifiers are **restrictive** and do not require commas.

If only one woman is standing in the back row, *wearing the pink hat* is extra information and not necessary to identify your aunt. The modifier in this case is **nonrestrictive** and is set off by commas.

Distinguish restrictive and nonrestrictive modifiers

You can distinguish between restrictive and nonrestrictive modifiers by deleting the modifier and then deciding whether the remaining sentence is changed. For example, delete the modifier *still stained by its bloody Tiananmen Square crackdown* from the following sentence:

> Some members of the Olympic Site Selection Committee wanted to prevent China, **still stained by its bloody Tianamen Square crackdown**, from hosting the 2008 games.

The result leaves the meaning of the main clause unchanged.

> Some members of the Olympic Site Selection Committee wanted to prevent China from hosting the 2008 games.

The modifier is nonrestrictive and should be set off by commas.

Pay special attention to appositives

Clauses and phrases can be restrictive or nonrestrictive, depending on the context. Often the difference is obvious, but some modifiers require close

consideration, especially appositives. An **appositive** is a noun or noun phrase that identifies or adds information to the noun preceding it.

Consider the following pair.

1 The world's most popular music players iPods changed the way people purchase and listen to music.

2 The world's most popular music players, iPods, changed the way people purchase and listen to music.

Which is correct? The appositive *iPods* is not essential to the meaning of the sentence and offers additional information. Sentence 2 is correct.

Use commas to mark off parenthetical expressions

A **parenthetical expression** provides information or commentary that usually is not essential to the sentence's meaning.

Incorrect My mother much to my surprise didn't say anything when she saw my pierced nose.

Correct My mother, much to my surprise, didn't say anything when she saw my pierced nose.

29d Commas with Items in a Series

In a series of three or more items, place a comma after each item except the last one. The comma between the last two items goes before the conjunction (*and, or*).

Health officials in Trenton, Manhattan, and the Bronx have all reported new cases of the West Nile virus.

29e Commas with Coordinate Adjectives

Coordinate adjectives are two or more adjectives that modify the same noun independently. Coordinate adjectives that are not linked by *and* must be separated by a comma.

After the NASDAQ bubble burst in 2000 and 2001, the Internet technology companies that remained were no longer the fresh-faced, giddy kids of Wall Street.

You can recognize coordinate adjectives by reversing their order; if their meaning remains the same, the adjectives are coordinate and must be linked by *and* or separated by a comma.

Commas are not used between **cumulative adjectives**. Cumulative adjectives are two or more adjectives that work together to modify a noun: *deep blue sea, inexpensive mountain bike.* If reversing their order changes the description of the noun (or violates the order of English, such as *mountain inexpensive bike*), the adjectives are cumulative and should not be separated by a comma.

The following example doesn't require a comma in the cumulative adjective series *massive Corinthian.*

Visitors to Rome's Pantheon pass between the massive Corinthian columns flanking the front door.

We know they are cumulative because reversing their order to read *Corinthian massive* would alter the way they modify *columns*—in this case, so much so that they no longer make sense.

29f Commas with Quotations

Properly punctuating quotations with commas can be tricky unless you know a few rules about when and where to use commas.

When to use commas with quotations

Commas set off phrases that attribute quotations to a speaker or writer, such as *he argues, they said,* and *she writes.*

"When you come to a fork in the road," said Yogi Berra, "take it!"

If the attribution follows a quotation that is a complete sentence, replace the period that would normally come at the end of the quotation with a comma.

Incorrect "Simplicity of language is not only reputable but perhaps even sacred." writes Kurt Vonnegut.

Correct "Simplicity of language is not only reputable but perhaps even sacred," writes Kurt Vonnegut.

When an attribution is placed in the middle of a quoted sentence, put the comma preceding the attribution within the quotation mark just before the phrase.

When not to use commas with quotations

Do not replace a question mark or exclamation point with a comma.

Incorrect "Who's on first," Costello asked Abbott.

Correct "Who's on first?" Costello asked Abbott.

Not all phrases that mention the author's name are attributions. When quoting a term or using a quotation within a subordinate clause, do not set off the quotation with commas.

> "Stonewall" Jackson gained his nickname at the First Battle of Bull Run when General Barnard Bee shouted to his men that Jackson was "standing like a stone wall."

29g Commas with Dates, Numbers, Titles, and Addresses

Some of the easiest comma rules to remember are the ones we use every day in dates, numbers, personal titles, place names, direct address, and brief interjections.

Commas with dates

Use commas to separate the day of the week from the month and to set off a year from the rest of the sentence.

> Monday, November 18, 2002

> On July 27, 2012, the opening ceremony of the World Scout Jamboree will be televised.

Do not use a comma when the month immediately precedes the year.

April 2010

Commas with numbers

Commas mark off thousands, millions, billions, and so on.

16,500,000

However, do not use commas in street addresses or page numbers.

page 1542

7602 Elm Street

Commas with personal titles

When a title follows a person's name, set the title off with commas.

Gregory House, MD

Commas with place names

Place a comma between street addresses, city names, state names, and countries.

Write to the president at 1600 Pennsylvania Avenue, Washington, DC 20500.

Commas in direct address

When addressing someone directly, set off that person's name in commas.

I was happy to get your letter yesterday, Jamie.

Commas with brief interjections

Use commas to set off brief interjections like *yes* and *no,* as well as short questions that fall at the ends of sentences.

Have another piece of pie, won't you?

29h Commas to Avoid Confusion

Certain sentences can confuse readers if you do not indicate where they should pause within the sentence. Use a comma to guide a reader through these usually compact constructions.

Unclear With supplies low prices of gasoline and fuel oil will increase.

This sentence could be read as meaning *With supplies, low prices will increase.*

Clear With supplies low, prices of gasoline and fuel oil will increase.

29i Unnecessary Commas

Do not place a comma between a subject and the main verb.

Incorrect American children of immigrant parents, often do not speak their parents' native language.

Correct American children of immigrant parents often do not speak their parents' native language.

However, you do use commas to set off modifying phrases that separate subjects from verbs.

Correct Steven Pinker, author of *The Language Instinct*, argues that the ability to speak and understand language is an evolutionary adaptive trait.

Do not use a comma with a coordinating conjunction unless it joins two main clauses. (See the Common Errors box on page 218.)

Incorrect Susana thought finishing her first novel was hard, but soon learned that getting a publisher to buy it was much harder.

Correct Susana thought finishing her first novel was hard but soon learned that getting a publisher to buy it was much harder.

Correct Susana thought finishing her first novel was hard, but she soon learned that getting a publisher to buy it was much harder.

Do not use a comma after a subordinating conjunction such as *although*, *despite*, or *while*.

Incorrect Although, soccer is gaining popularity in the States, it will never be as popular as football or baseball.

Correct Although soccer is gaining popularity in the States, it will never be as popular as football or baseball.

Some writers mistakenly use a comma with *than* to try to heighten the contrast in a comparison.

Incorrect Any teacher will tell you that acquiring critical thinking skills is more important, than simply memorizing information.

Correct Any teacher will tell you that acquiring critical thinking skills is more important than simply memorizing information.

A common mistake is to place a comma after *such as* or *like* before introducing a list.

Incorrect Many hourly workers, such as, waiters, dishwashers, and cashiers, do not receive health benefits from their employers.

Correct Many hourly workers, such as waiters, dishwashers, and cashiers, do not receive health benefits from their employers.

30 Semicolons and Colons

Semicolons and colons link closely related ideas.

30a Semicolons with Closely Related Main Clauses

Why use semicolons? Sometimes we want to join two main clauses to form a complete sentence in order to indicate their close relationship. We can connect them with a comma and a coordinating conjunction like *or, but,* or

and. To create variation in sentence style and avoid wordiness, we can omit the comma and coordinating conjunction and insert a semicolon between the two clauses.

Semicolons can join only clauses that are grammatically equal. In other words, they join main clauses only to other main clauses, not to phrases or subordinate clauses. Look at the following examples:

Incorrect [MAIN CLAUSE: Gloria's new weightlifting program will help her recover from knee surgery]; [PHRASE: doing a series of squats and presses with a physical therapist].

Correct [MAIN CLAUSE: Gloria's new weightlifting program will help her recover from knee surgery]; [MAIN CLAUSE: a physical therapist leads her through a series of squats and presses].

COMMON ERRORS

Semicolons with transitional words and phrases

Closely related main clauses sometimes use a conjunctive adverb (such as *however, therefore, moreover, furthermore, thus, meanwhile, nonetheless, otherwise*) or a transitional phrase (*in fact, for example, that is, for instance, in addition, in other words, on the other hand, even so*) to indicate the relationship between them. When the second clause begins with a conjunctive adverb or a transitional phrase, a semicolon is needed to join the two clauses. This sentence pattern is frequently used; therefore, it pays to learn how to punctuate it correctly.

Incorrect (comma splice) The police and city officials want to crack down on drug use at raves, however, their efforts have been unsuccessful so far.

(Continued on next page)

COMMON ERRORS (continued)

Correct The police and city officials want to crack down on drug use at raves; however, their efforts have been unsuccessful so far.

Remember: Main clauses that use a conjunctive adverb or a transitional phrase require a semicolon to join the clauses.

Do not use a semicolon to introduce quotations

Use a comma or colon instead.

Incorrect Robert Frost's poem "Mending Wall" contains this line; "Good fences make good neighbors."

Correct Robert Frost's poem "Mending Wall" contains this line: "Good fences make good neighbors."

Do not use a semicolon to introduce lists

Incorrect William Shakespeare wrote four romance plays at the end of his career; *The Tempest, The Winter's Tale, Cymbeline,* and *Pericles.*

Correct William Shakespeare wrote four romance plays at the end of his career: *The Tempest, The Winter's Tale, Cymbeline,* and *Pericles.*

30b Semicolons Together with Commas

When an item in a series already includes a comma, adding more commas to separate it from the other items will only confuse the reader. Use semicolons instead of commas between items in a series that have internal punctuation.

Confusing The church's design competition drew entries from as far away as Gothenberg, Sweden, Caracas, Venezuela, and Athens, Greece.

Clearer The church's design competition drew entries from as far away as Gothenberg, Sweden; Caracas, Venezuela; and Athens, Greece.

30c Colons in Sentences

Like semicolons, colons can join two closely related main clauses (complete sentences). Colons indicate that what follows will explain or expand on what comes before the colon. Use a colon in cases where the second main clause interprets or sums up the first.

> The sighting of a South China tiger in 2007 proved they are not extinct in the wild, but the outlook for their survival is not optimistic: the genetic diversity required to maintain the subspecies has been lost.

You may choose to capitalize the first word of the main clause following the colon or leave it lowercase. Either is correct as long as you are consistent throughout your text.

Colons linking main clauses with appositives

A colon calls attention to an appositive, a noun, or a noun phrase that renames the noun preceding it. If you're not certain whether a colon would be appropriate, put *namely* in its place. If *namely* makes sense when you read the main clause followed by the appositive, you probably need to insert a colon instead of a comma. Remember, the clause that precedes the colon must be a complete sentence.

> I know the perfect person for the job, namely me.

The sentence makes sense with *namely* placed before the appositive. Thus, a colon is appropriate.

> I know the perfect person for the job: me.

Never capitalize a word following a colon unless the word starts a complete sentence or is normally capitalized.

Colons joining main clauses with quotations

Use a colon to link a main clause and a quotation that interprets or sums up the clause. Be careful not to use a colon to link a phrase with a quotation.

Incorrect: phrase–colon–quotation

President Roosevelt's strategy to change the nation's panicky attitude during the Great Depression: "We have nothing to fear," he said, "but fear itself."

Correct: main clause–colon–quotation

President Roosevelt's strategy to end the Great Depression was to change the nation's panicky attitude: "We have nothing to fear," he said, "but fear itself."

The first example is incorrect because there is no main verb in the first part of the sentence and thus it is a phrase rather than a main clause. The second example adds the verb (*was*), making the first part of the sentence a main clause.

30d Colons with Lists

Use a colon to join a main clause to a list. The main clauses in these cases sometimes include the phrase *the following* or *as follows.* Remember that a colon cannot join a phrase or an incomplete clause to a list.

Incorrect: phrase–colon–list

Three posters decorating Juan's apartment: an old Santana concert poster, a view of Mount Rainier, and a Diego Rivera mural.

Correct: main clause–colon–list

Juan bought three posters to decorate his apartment: an old Santana concert poster, a view of Mount Rainier, and a Diego Rivera mural.

COMMON ERRORS

Colons misused with lists

Some writers think that anytime they introduce a list, they should insert a colon. Colons are used correctly only when a complete sentence precedes the colon.

Incorrect Jessica's entire wardrobe for her trip to Cancun included: two swimsuits, one pair of shorts, two T-shirts, a party dress, and a pair of sandals.

Correct Jessica's entire wardrobe for her trip to Cancun included two swimsuits, one pair of shorts, two T-shirts, a party dress, and a pair of sandals.

Correct Jessica jotted down what she would need for her trip: two swimsuits, one pair of shorts, two T-shirts, a party dress, and a pair of sandals.

Remember: A colon should be placed only after a clause that can stand by itself as a sentence.

31 Dashes and Parentheses

Dashes and parentheses call attention to information that comments on your ideas.

31a Dashes and Parentheses to Set Off Information

Dashes and parentheses call attention to groups of words. In effect, they tell the reader that a group of words is not part of the main clause and should be given extra attention. If you want to make an element stand out, especially in the middle of a sentence, use parentheses or dashes instead of commas.

Dashes with final elements

A dash is often used to set off a phrase or subordinate clause at the end of a sentence to offer a significant comment about the main clause. Dashes can also anticipate a shift in tone at the end of a sentence.

> A full-sized SUV can take you wherever you want to go in style—if your idea of style is a gas-guzzling tank.

Parentheses with additional information

Parentheses are more often used for identifying information, afterthoughts or asides, examples, and clarifications. You can place full sentences, fragments, or brief terms within parentheses.

> Some argue that ethanol (the pet solution of politicians for achieving energy independence) costs more energy to manufacture and ship than it produces.

COMMON ERRORS

Do not use dashes as periods

Do not use dashes to separate two main clauses (clauses that can stand as complete sentences). Use dashes to separate main clauses from subordinate clauses and phrases when you want to emphasize the subordinate clause or phrase.

Incorrect: main clause–dash–main clause

> I was one of the few women in my computer science classes—most of the students majoring in computer science at that time were men.

COMMON ERRORS (continued)

Correct: main clause–dash–phrase

I was one of the few women in computer science—a field then dominated by men.

Remember: Dashes are not periods and should not be used as periods.

31b Dashes and Parentheses versus Commas

Like commas, parentheses and dashes enclose material that adds, explains, or digresses. However, the three punctuation marks are not interchangeable. The mark you choose depends on how much emphasis you want to place on the material. Dashes indicate the most emphasis. Parentheses offer somewhat less, and commas offer less still.

Commas indicate a moderate level of emphasis

Bill covered the new tattoo on his bicep, a pouncing tiger, because he thought it might upset our mother.

Parentheses lend a greater level of emphasis

I'm afraid to go bungee jumping (though my brother tells me it's less frightening than a roller coaster).

Dashes indicate the highest level of emphasis and, sometimes, surprise and drama

Christina felt as though she had been punched in the gut; she could hardly believe the stranger at her door was really who he claimed to be—the brother she hadn't seen in twenty years.

COMMON ERRORS

The art of typing a dash

Although dashes and hyphens may look similar, they are actually different marks. The distinction is small but important because dashes and hyphens serve different purposes. A dash is a line twice as long as a hyphen. Most word processors will create a dash automatically when you type two hyphens together. Or you can type a special character to make a dash. Your manual will tell you which keys to press to make a dash.

Do not leave a space between a dash or a hyphen and the words that come before and after them. Likewise, if you are using two hyphens to indicate a dash, do not leave a space between the hyphens.

Incorrect A well - timed effort at conserving water may prevent long - term damage to drought - stricken farms -- if it's not already too late.

Correct A well-timed effort at conserving water may prevent long-term damage to drought-stricken farms—if it's not already too late.

Remember: Do not put spaces before or after hyphens and dashes.

31c Other Punctuation with Parentheses

Parentheses around letters or numbers that order a series within a sentence make the list easier to read.

> Angela Creider's recipe for becoming a great novelist is to (1) set aside an hour during the morning to write, (2) read what you've written out loud, (3) revise your prose, and (4) repeat every morning for the next thirty years.

Abbreviations made from the first letters of words are often used in place of the unwieldy names of institutions, departments, organizations, or terms. In order to show the reader what the abbreviation stands for, the first time it appears in a text the writer must state the complete name, followed by the abbreviation in parentheses.

> The University of California, Santa Cruz (UCSC) supports its mascot, the banana slug, with pride and a sense of humor. And although it sounds strange to outsiders, UCSC students are even referred to as "the banana slugs."

COMMON ERRORS

Using periods, commas, colons, and semicolons with parentheses

When an entire sentence is enclosed in parentheses, place the period before the closing parenthesis.

Incorrect Our fear of sharks, heightened by movies like *Jaws*, is vastly out of proportion with the minor threat sharks actually pose. (Dying from a dog attack, in fact, is much more likely than dying from a shark attack).

Correct Our fear of sharks, heightened by movies like *Jaws*, is vastly out of proportion with the minor threat sharks actually pose. (Dying from a dog attack, in fact, is much more likely than dying from a shark attack.)

When the material in parentheses is part of the sentence and the parentheses fall at the end of the sentence, place the period outside the closing parenthesis.

(Continued on next page)

COMMON ERRORS (continued)

Incorrect Reports of sharks attacking people are rare (much rarer than dog attacks.)

Correct Reports of sharks attacking people are rare (much rarer than dog attacks).

Place commas, colons, and semicolons after the closing parenthesis.

Remember: When an entire sentence is enclosed in parentheses, place the period inside the closing parenthesis; otherwise, put the punctuation outside the closing parenthesis.

32 Apostrophes

Apostrophes indicate possession, mark contractions, and form certain plurals.

32a Possessives

Nouns and indefinite pronouns (for example, *everyone, anyone*) that indicate possession or ownership are marked by attaching an apostrophe and *-s* or an apostrophe only to the end of the word.

Singular nouns and indefinite pronouns

For singular nouns and indefinite pronouns, add an apostrophe plus *-s: -'s*. Even singular nouns that end in *-s* usually follow this principle.

Iris's coat

everyone's favorite

a woman's choice

There are a few exceptions to adding *-'s* for singular nouns:

- **Awkward pronunciations** *Herodotus' travels, Jesus' sermons*
- **Official names of certain places, institutions, companies** *Governors Island, Teachers College of Columbia University, Mothers Café, Saks Fifth Avenue, Walgreens Pharmacy.* Note, however, that many companies do include the apostrophe: *Denny's Restaurant, Macy's, McDonald's, Wendy's Old Fashioned Hamburgers.*

Plural nouns

For plural nouns that do not end in *-s*, add an apostrophe plus *-s: -'s.*

media's responsibility

children's section

For plural nouns that end in *-s*, add only an apostrophe at the end.

attorneys' briefs

the Kennedys' legacy

Compound nouns

For compound nouns, add an apostrophe plus *-s* to the last word of the compound noun: *-'s.*

mayor of Cleveland's speech

Two or more nouns

For joint possession, add an apostrophe plus *-s* to the final noun: *-'s.*

mother and dad's yard

When people possess or own things separately, add an apostrophe plus *-s* to each noun: *-'s.*

Roberto's and Edward's views are totally opposed.

COMMON ERRORS

Possessive forms of personal pronouns never take the apostrophe

Incorrect *her's, it's, our's, your's, their's*

The bird sang in **it's** cage.

Correct *hers, its, ours, yours, theirs*

The bird sang in **its** cage.

Remember: ***It's = It is***

32b Contractions and Omitted Letters

In speech we often leave out sounds and syllables of familiar words. These omissions are noted with apostrophes.

Contractions

Contractions combine two words into one, using the apostrophe to mark what is left out.

I am → I'm
I would → I'd
you are → you're
you will → you'll
he is → he's
she is → she's
it is → it's

we are → we're
they are → they're
cannot → can't
do not → don't
does not → doesn't
will not → won't

Omissions

Using apostrophes to signal omitted letters is a way of approximating speech in writing. They can make your writing look informal and slangy, and overuse can become annoying in a hurry.

rock and roll ——→ rock 'n' roll
the 1960s ——→ the '60s
neighborhood ——→ 'hood

32c Plurals of Letters, Symbols, and Words Referred to as Words

When to use apostrophes to make plurals

The trend is away from using apostrophes to form plurals of letters, symbols, and words referred to as words. Most readers now prefer 1960s to the older form, 1960's. In a few cases adding the apostrophe and *s* is still used, as in this old saying:

> Mind your p's and q's.

Words used as words are italicized and their plural is formed by adding an *s* not in italics, not an apostrophe and *s*.

> Take a few of the *and*s out of your writing.

Words in quotation marks, however, typically use apostrophe and *s*.

> She had too many "probably's" in her letter for me to be confident that the remodeling will be finished on schedule.

When not to use apostrophes to make plurals

Do not use an apostrophe to make family names plural.

Incorrect You've heard of keeping up with the Jones's.

Correct You've heard of keeping up with the Joneses.

COMMON ERRORS

Do not use an apostrophe to make a noun plural

Incorrect The two government's agreed to meet.

Correct The two governments agreed to meet.

Incorrect The video game console's of the past were one-dimensional.

Correct The video game consoles of the past were one-dimensional.

Remember: Add only *-s* = plural
Add apostrophe plus *-s* = possessive

33 Quotation Marks

Quotation marks perform several functions.

33a Direct Quotations

Use quotation marks to enclose direct quotations

Enclose direct quotations—someone else's words repeated verbatim—in quotation marks.

> Dan Glickman, CEO of the MPAA, the organization that rates U.S. films, argues that smoking is enough of a concern to parents that it should be considered when assigning movie ratings: "There is broad awareness of smoking as a unique public health concern due to nicotine's highly addictive nature, and no parent wants their child to take up the habit. The

appropriate response of the rating system is to give more information to parents on this issue."

Do not use quotation marks with indirect quotations

Do not enclose an indirect quotation—a paraphrase of someone else's words—in quotation marks. However, do remember that you need to cite your source not only when you quote directly but also when you paraphrase or borrow ideas.

> Dan Glickman of the MPAA thinks that because parents don't want their children to start smoking, they should be warned when movies contain scenes where characters smoke (98).

Do not use quotation marks with block quotations

When a quotation is long enough to be set off as a block quotation, do not use quotation marks. MLA style defines long quotations as more than four lines of prose or poetry. APA style defines a long quotation as one of more than forty words.

In the following example, notice that the long quotation is indented and quotation marks are omitted. Also notice that the parenthetical citation for a long quotation comes after the period.

> Complaints about maintenance in the dorms have been on the rise ever since the physical plant reorganized its crews into teams in August. One student's experience is typical:
>
> > When our ceiling started dripping, my roommate and I went to our resident director right away to file an emergency maintenance request. Apparently the physical plant felt that "emergency" meant they could get around to it in a week or two. By the fourth day without any word from a maintenance person, the ceiling tiles began to fall and puddles began to pool on our carpet. (Trillo)
>
> The physical plant could have avoided expensive ceiling tile and carpet repairs if it had responded to the student's request promptly.

33b Titles of Short Works

While the titles of longer works such as books, magazines, and newspapers are italicized or underlined, titles of shorter works should be set off with quotation marks. Use quotation marks with the following kinds of titles:

Short stories	"Light Is Like Water," by Gabriel García Márquez
Magazine articles	"Race against Death," by Erin West
Newspaper articles	"Cincinnati Mayor Declares Emergency," by Liz Sidoti
Short poems	"We Real Cool," by Gwendolyn Brooks
Essays	"Self-Reliance," by Ralph Waldo Emerson

The exception. Don't put the title of your own paper in quotation marks. If the title of another short work appears within the title of your paper, retain the quotation marks around the short work.

33c Other Uses of Quotation Marks

Quotation marks around a term can indicate that the writer is using the term in a novel way, often with skepticism, irony, or sarcasm. The quotation marks indicate that the writer is questioning the term's conventional definition.

Italics are usually used to indicate that a word is being used as a word, rather than standing for its conventional meaning. However, quotation marks are correct in these cases as well.

> Beginning writers sometimes confuse "their," "they're," and "there."

33d Other Punctuation with Quotation Marks

The rules for placing punctuation with quotation marks fall into three general categories.

Periods and commas with quotation marks

Place periods and commas inside closing quotation marks.

Incorrect "The smartest people", Dr. Geisler pointed out, "tell themselves the most convincing rationalizations".

Correct "The smartest people," Dr. Geisler pointed out, "tell themselves the most convincing rationalizations."

Colons and semicolons with quotation marks

Place colons and semicolons outside closing quotation marks.

Incorrect "From Stettin in the Baltic to Trieste in the Adriatic, an iron curtain has descended across the Continent;" Churchill's statement rang through Cold War politics for the next fifty years.

Correct "From Stettin in the Baltic to Trieste in the Adriatic, an iron curtain has descended across the Continent"; Churchill's statement rang through Cold War politics for the next fifty years.

Exclamation points, question marks, and dashes with quotation marks

When an exclamation point, question mark, or dash belongs to the original quotation, place it inside the closing quotation mark. When it applies to the entire sentence, place it outside the closing quotation mark.

In the original quotation

"Are we there yet?" came the whine from the back seat.

Applied to the entire sentence

Did the driver in the front seat respond, "Not even close"?

COMMON ERRORS

Quotations within quotations

Single quotation marks are used to indicate a quotation within a quotation. In the following example single quotation marks clarify who is speaking. The rules for placing punctuation with single quotation marks are the same as the rules for placing punctuation with double quotation marks.

Incorrect When he showed the report to Paul Probius, Michener reported that Probius "took vigorous exception to the sentence "He wanted to close down the university," insisting that we add the clarifying phrase "as it then existed"" (Michener 145).

Correct When he showed the report to Paul Probius, Michener reported that Probius "took vigorous exception to the sentence 'He wanted to close down the university,' insisting that we add the clarifying phrase 'as it then existed'" (Michener 145).

Remember: Single quotation marks are used for quotations within quotations.

33e Misuses of Quotation Marks

It's becoming more and more common to see quotation marks used to emphasize a word or phrase. Resist the temptation in your own writing; it's an incorrect usage. In fact, because quotation marks indicate that a writer is using a term with skepticism or irony, adding quotation marks for emphasis will highlight unintended connotations of the term.

Incorrect "fresh" seafood

By using quotation marks here, the writer seems to call into question whether the seafood is really fresh.

Correct fresh seafood

Incorrect Enjoy our "live" music every Saturday night.

Again, the quotation marks unintentionally indicate that the writer is skeptical that the music is live.

Correct Enjoy our live music every Saturday night.

You have better ways of creating emphasis using your word processing program: **boldfacing**, underlining, *italicizing*, and using color.

34 Other Punctuation Marks

Other punctuation marks are necessary for clarity.

34a Periods

Periods at the ends of sentences

Place a period at the end of a complete sentence if it is not a direct question or an exclamatory statement. As the term suggests, a direct question asks a question outright. Indirect questions, on the other hand, report the asking of a question.

Periods with quotation marks and parentheses

When a quotation falls at the end of a sentence, place the period inside the closing quotation marks.

> Although he devoted decades to a wide range of artistic and political projects, Allen Ginsberg is best known as the author of the poem "Howl."

When a parenthetical phrase falls at the end of a sentence, place the period outside the closing parenthesis. When parentheses enclose a whole sentence, place the period inside the closing parenthesis.

Periods with abbreviations

Many abbreviations require periods; however, there are few set rules. Use the dictionary to check how to punctuate abbreviations on a case-by-case basis. The rules for punctuating two types of abbreviations do remain consistent: Postal abbreviations for states and most abbreviations for organizations do not require periods. When an abbreviation with a period falls at the end of a sentence, do not add a second period to conclude the sentence.

Incorrect Her flight arrives at 6:22 p.m..

Correct Her flight arrives at 6:22 p.m.

Periods as decimal points

Decimal points are periods that separate integers from tenths, hundredths, and so on.

99.98% pure silver
on sale for $399.97
98.6° Fahrenheit
2.6 liter engine

Since large numbers with long strings of zeros can be difficult to read accurately, writers sometimes shorten them using decimal points. In this way, 16,600,000 can be written as 16.6 million.

34b Question Marks

Question marks with direct questions

Place a question mark at the end of a direct question. A direct question is one that the questioner puts to someone outright. In contrast, an indirect question merely reports the asking of a question. Question marks give readers a cue to read the end of the sentence with rising inflection. Read the

following sentences aloud. Hear how your inflection rises in the second sentence to convey the direct question.

Indirect question

Desirée asked whether Dan rides his motorcycle without a helmet.

Direct question

Desirée asked, "Does Dan ride his motorcycle without a helmet?"

Question marks with quotations

When a quotation falls at the end of a direct question, place the question mark outside the closing quotation mark.

> Did Abraham Lincoln really call Harriet Beecher Stowe "the little lady who started this big war"?

Place the question mark inside the closing quotation when only the quoted material is a direct question.

> Slowly scientists are beginning to answer the question, "Is cancer a genetic disease?"

When quoting a direct question in the middle of a sentence, place a question mark inside the closing quotation mark and place a period at the end of the sentence.

> Market researchers estimate that asking Burger World's customers "Do you want fries with that?" is responsible for a 15% boost in their french fries sales.

34c Exclamation Points

Exclamation points to convey strong emotion

Exclamation points conclude sentences and, like question marks, tell the reader how a sentence should sound. They indicate strong emotion. Use exclamation points sparingly in formal writing; they are rarely appropriate in academic and professional prose.

Exclamation points with emphatic interjections

Exclamation points can convey a sense of urgency with brief interjections. Interjections can be incorporated into sentences or stand on their own.

> Run! They're about to close the doors to the jetway.

Exclamation points with quotation marks

In quotations, exclamation points follow the same rules as question marks. If a quotation falls at the end of an exclamatory statement, place the exclamation point outside the closing quotation mark.

> The singer forgot the words to "America the Beautiful"!

When quoting an exclamatory statement at the end of a sentence that is not itself exclamatory, place the exclamation point inside the closing quotation mark.

> Jerry thought his car would be washed away in the flood, but Anna jumped into action, declaring, "Not if I can help it!"

34d Brackets

While brackets (sometimes called *square brackets*) look quite similar to parentheses, the two perform different functions. Brackets have a narrow set of uses.

Brackets to provide clarification within quotation marks

Use brackets if you are interjecting a comment of your own or clarifying information within a direct quotation. In the following example the writer quotes a sentence with the pronoun *they,* which refers to a noun in a previous, unquoted sentence. The material in brackets clarifies to whom the pronoun refers.

> The Harris study found that "In the last three years, they [Gonzales Junior High students] averaged 15% higher on their mathematics assessment tests than their peers in Northridge County."

Brackets within parentheses

Since parentheses within parentheses might confuse readers, use brackets to enclose parenthetical information within a parenthetical phrase.

> Representative Patel's most controversial legislation (including a version of the hate crimes bill [HR 99-108] the house rejected two years ago) has a slim chance of being enacted this session.

34e Ellipses

Ellipses let a reader know that a portion of a passage is missing. You can use ellipses to keep quotations concise and direct readers' attention to what is important to the point you are making. An ellipsis is a string of three periods with spaces separating the periods.

Ellipses to indicate an omission from a quotation

When you quote only a phrase or short clause from a sentence, you usually do not need to use ellipses.

> Mao Zedong first used "let a hundred flowers blossom" in a Beijing speech in 1957.

Except at the beginning of a quotation, indicate omitted words with an ellipsis.

The original source

> "The female praying mantis, so named for the way it holds its front legs together as if in prayer, tears off her male partner's head during mating. Remarkably, the headless male will continue the act of mating. This brutal dance is a stark example of the innate evolutionary drive to pass genes onto offspring; the male praying mantis seems to live and die only for this moment."

An ellipsis indicates omitted words

> "The female praying mantis . . . tears off her male partner's head during mating."

When the ellipsis is at the end of a sentence, place the period or question mark after the ellipsis and follow with the closing quotation mark.

Words omitted at the end of a sentence

> "This brutal dance is a stark example of the innate evolutionary drive to pass genes onto offspring. . . ."

34f Slashes

Slashes to indicate alternative words

Slashes between two words indicate that a choice between them is to be made. When using slashes for this purpose, do not put a space between the slash and words.

Incorrect Maya was such an energetic baby that her exhausted parents wished she had come with an on / off switch.

Correct Maya was such an energetic baby that her exhausted parents wished she had come with an on/off switch.

Slashes with fractions

Place a slash between the numerator and the denominator in a fraction. Do not put any spaces around the slash.

Incorrect 3 / 4

Correct 3/4

35 Capitalization, Italics, Abbreviations, Numbers

Different kinds of writing follow specific conventions.

35a Capital Letters

Capitalize the initial letters of proper nouns (nouns that name particular people, places, and things). Capitalize the initial letters of proper adjectives (adjectives based on the names of people, places, and things).

African American bookstore   Avogadro's number   Irish music

Do not capitalize the names of seasons, academic disciplines (unless they are languages), or job titles used without a proper noun.

35b Italics

Italicize the titles of entire works (books, magazines, newspapers, films), but place the titles of parts of entire works within quotation marks. Also italicize or underline the names of ships and aircraft.

I am fond of reading *USA Today* in the morning.

The exceptions. Do not italicize or underline the names of sacred texts.

Italicize unfamiliar foreign words

Italicize foreign words that are not part of common English usage. Do not italicize words that have become a common word or phrase in the English vocabulary. How do you decide which words are common? If a word appears in a standard English dictionary, it can be considered as adopted into English.

Use italics to clarify your use of a word, letter, or number

In everyday speech, we often use cues—a pause, a louder or different tone—to communicate how we are using a word. In writing, italics help clarify when you use words in a referential manner, or letters and numbers as letters and numbers.

35c Abbreviations

Abbreviations are shortened forms of words. Because abbreviations vary widely, you will need to look in the dictionary to determine how to abbreviate words on a case-by-case basis. Nonetheless, there are a few patterns that abbreviations follow.

Abbreviate titles before and degrees after full names

Ms. Ella Fitzgerald

Prof. Vijay Aggarwal

Write out the professional title when it is used with only a last name.

Professor Chin

Reverend Ames

Conventions for using abbreviations with years and times

BCE (before the common era) and CE (common era) are now preferred for indicating years, replacing BC (before Christ) and AD (*anno Domini* ["the year of our Lord"]). Note that all are now used without periods.

479 BCE (or BC)

1610 CE (or AD, but AD is placed before the number)

The preferred written conventions for times are a.m. (*ante meridiem*) and p.m. (*post meridiem*).

9:03 a.m.

3:30 p.m.

Conventions for using abbreviations in formal writing

Most abbreviations are inappropriate in formal writing except when the reader would be more familiar with the abbreviation than with the words it represents. When your reader is unlikely to be familiar with an abbreviation, spell out the term, followed by the abbreviation in parentheses, the first time you use it in a paper. The reader will then understand what the abbreviation refers to, and you may use the abbreviation in subsequent sentences.

> The **Office of Civil Rights (OCR)** is the agency that enforces Title IX regulations. In 1979, **OCR** set out three options for schools to comply with Title IX.

35d Acronyms

Acronyms are abbreviations formed by capitalizing the first letter in each word. Unlike abbreviations, acronyms are pronounced as words.

> **AIDS** for Acquired Immunodeficiency Syndrome
>
> **NASA** for National Air and Space Administration

A subset of acronyms are initial-letter abbreviations that have become so common that we know the organization or thing by its initials.

> **ACLU** for American Civil Liberties Union
>
> **HIV** for human immunodeficiency virus
>
> **rpm** for revolutions per minute

Familiar acronyms and initial-letter abbreviations such as CBS, CIA, FBI, IQ, and UN are rarely spelled out. Unfamiliar acronyms and abbreviations should always be spelled out. Acronyms and abbreviations frequent in particular fields should be spelled out on first use. For example, MMPI (Minnesota Multiphasic Personality Inventory) is a familiar abbreviation in psychology but is unfamiliar to those outside that discipline. Even when acronyms are generally familiar, few readers will object to your giving the terms from which an acronym derives on the first use.

35e Numbers

In formal writing spell out any number that can be expressed in one or two words, as well as any number, regardless of length, at the beginning of a sentence. Also, hyphenate two-word numbers from twenty-one to ninety-nine. When a sentence begins with a number that requires more than two words, revise it if possible.

The exceptions. In scientific reports and some business writing that requires the frequent use of numbers, using numerals more often is appropriate. Most styles do not write out in words a year, a date, an address, a page number, the time of day, decimals, sums of money, phone numbers, rates of speed, or the scene and act of a play. Use numerals instead.

> In 2001 only 33% of respondents said they were satisfied with the City Council's proposals to help the homeless.

> The 17 trials were conducted at temperatures 12-14°C with results ranging from 2.43 to 2.89 mg/dl.

When one number modifies another number, write one out and express the other in numeral form.

> In the last year all four 8th Street restaurants have begun to donate their leftovers to the soup kitchen.

> Only after Meryl had run in 12 fifty-mile ultramarathons did she finally win first place in her age group.

Glossary of Grammatical Terms and Usage

The glossary gives the definitions of grammatical terms and items of usage. The grammatical terms are shown in **blue**. Some of the explanations of usage that follow are not rules, but guidelines to keep in mind for academic and professional writing. In these formal contexts, the safest course is to avoid words that are described as *nonstandard, informal,* or *colloquial.*

a/an Use *a* before words that begin with a consonant sound (*a train, a house*). Use *an* before words that begin with a vowel sound (*an airplane, an hour*).

a lot/alot *A lot* is generally regarded as informal; *alot* is nonstandard.

accept/except *Accept* is a verb meaning "receive" or "approve." *Except* is sometimes a verb meaning "leave out," but much more often it's used as a conjunction or preposition meaning "other than."

active A clause with a transitive verb in which the subject is the doer of the action (see Section 18a). See also **passive.**

adjective A modifier that qualifies or describes the qualities of a noun or pronoun (see Sections 27a and 27b).

adjective clause A subordinate clause that modifies a noun or pronoun and is usually introduced by a relative pronoun (see Section 27b). Sometimes called a *relative clause.*

adverb A word that modifies a verb, another modifier, or a clause (see Sections 27a and 27c).

adverb clause A subordinate clause that functions as an adverb by modifying a verb, another modifier, or a clause (see Section 27c).

advice/advise The noun *advice* means a "suggestion"; the verb *advise* means to "recommend" or "give advice."

affect/effect Usually, *affect* is a verb (to "influence") and *effect* is a noun (a "result"). Less commonly, *affect* is used as a noun and *effect* as a verb.

agreement The number and person of a subject and verb must match—singular subjects with singular verbs, plural subjects with plural verbs (see Chapter 23). Likewise, the number and gender of a pronoun and its antecedent must match (see Section 25b).

all ready/already The adjective phrase *all ready* means "completely prepared"; the adverb *already* means "previously."

all right/alright *All right,* meaning "acceptable," is the correct spelling. *Alright* is nonstandard.

allude/elude *Allude* means "refer to indirectly." *Elude* means "evade."

allusion/illusion An *allusion* is an indirect reference; an *illusion* is a false impression.

among/between *Between* refers to precisely two people or things; *among* refers to three or more.

amount/number Use *amount* with things that cannot be counted; use *number* with things that can be counted.

an See **a/an.**

antecedent The noun (or pronoun) that a pronoun refers to (see Section 25b).

anybody/any body; anyone/any one *Anybody* and *anyone* are indefinite pronouns and have the same meaning. In *any body, body* is a noun modified by *any,* and in *any one, one* is a pronoun or adjective modified by *any.*

anymore/any more *Anymore* means "now," while *any more* means "no more." Both are used in negative constructions.

anyway/anyways *Anyway* is correct. *Anyways* is nonstandard.

articles The words *a, an,* and *the* (see Section 28b).

as/as if/as though/like Use *as* instead of *like* before dependent clauses (which include a subject and verb). Use *like* before a noun or a pronoun.

assure/ensure/insure *Assure* means "promise," *ensure* means "make certain," and *insure* means to "make certain in either a legal or financial sense."

auxiliary verb Forms of *be, do,* and *have* combine with verbs to indicate tense and mood (see Section 28c). The modal verbs *can, could, may, might, must, shall, should, will,* and *would* are a subset of auxiliaries.

bad/badly Use *bad* only as an adjective. *Badly* is the adverb.

being as/being that Both constructions are colloquial and awkward substitutes for *because.* Don't use them in formal writing.

beside/besides *Beside* means "next to." *Besides* means "in addition to" or "except."

between See **among/between.**

bring/take *Bring* describes movement from a more distant location to a nearer one. *Take* describes movement away.

can/may In formal writing, *can* indicates ability or capacity, while *may* indicates permission.

case The form of a noun or pronoun that indicates its function. Nouns change case only to show possession: the **dog**, the **dog's** bowl. See **pronoun case** (Section 25a).

censor/censure To *censor* is to edit or ban on moral or political grounds. To *censure* is to reprimand publicly.

cite/sight/site To *cite* is to "mention specifically"; *sight* as a verb means to "observe" and as a noun refers to "vision"; *site* is most commonly used as a noun that means "location," but it is also used as a verb to mean "situate."

clause A group of words with a subject and a predicate. A main or independent clause can stand as a sentence. A subordinate or dependent clause must be attached to a main clause to form a sentence (see Section 22a).

collective noun A noun that refers to a group or a plurality, such as *team, army,* or *committee* (see Section 23d).

comma splice Two independent clauses joined incorrectly by a comma (see Section 22c).

common noun A noun that names a general group, person, place, or thing (see Section 28a). Common nouns are not capitalized unless they begin a sentence.

complement A word or group of words that completes the predicate. See also **linking verb.**

complement/compliment To *complement* something is to complete it or make it perfect; to *compliment* is to flatter.

complex sentence A sentence that contains at least one subordinate clause attached to a main clause.

compound sentence A sentence that contains at least two main clauses.

compound-complex sentence A sentence that contains at least two main clauses and one subordinate clause.

conjunction See **coordinating conjunction** and **subordinating conjunction.**

conjunctive adverb An adverb that often modifies entire clauses and sentences, such as *also, consequently, however, indeed, instead, moreover, nevertheless, otherwise, similarly,* and *therefore* (see Section 27c).

continual/continuous *Continual* refers to a repeated activity; *continuous* refers to an ongoing, unceasing activity.

coordinate A relationship of equal importance, in terms of either grammar or meaning (see Section 20c).

coordinating conjunction A word that links two equivalent grammatical elements, such as *and, but, or, yet, nor, for,* and *so.*

could of Nonstandard. See **have/of.**

count noun A noun that names things that can be counted, such as *block, cat,* and *toy* (see Section 28a).

dangling modifier A modifier that is not clearly attached to what it modifies (see Section 27e).

data The plural form of *datum*; it takes plural verb forms.

declarative A sentence that makes a statement.

dependent clause See **subordinate clause.**

determiners Words that initiate noun phrases, including possessive nouns (*Pedro's*); possessive pronouns (*my, your*); demonstrative pronouns (*this, that*); and indefinite pronouns (*all, both, many*).

differ from/differ with To *differ from* means to "be unlike"; to *differ with* means to "disagree."

different from/different than Use *different from* where possible.

Dark French roast is **different from** ordinary coffee.

direct object A noun, pronoun, or noun clause that names who or what receives the action of a transitive verb.

discreet/discrete Both are adjectives. *Discreet* means "prudent" or "tactful"; *discrete* means "separate."

disinterested/uninterested *Disinterested* is often misused to mean *uninterested.* Disinterested means "impartial." A judge can be interested in a case but disinterested in the outcome.

double negative The incorrect use of two negatives to signal the same negative meaning.

due to the fact that Avoid this wordy substitute for *because.*

each other/one another Use *each other* for two; use *one another* for more than two.

effect See **affect/effect**.

elicit/illicit The verb *elicit* means to "draw out." The adjective *illicit* means "unlawful."

emigrate from/immigrate to *Emigrate* means to "leave one's country"; *immigrate* means to "settle in another country."

ensure See **assure/ensure/insure**.

enthused Nonstandard in academic and professional writing. Use *enthusiastic* instead.

etc. Avoid this abbreviation for the Latin *et cetera* in formal writing. Either list all the items or use an English phrase such as *and so forth.*

every body/everybody; every one/everyone *Everybody* and *everyone* are indefinite pronouns referring to all people under discussion. *Every one* and *every body* are adjective-noun combinations referring to all members of a group.

except See **accept/except**.

except for the fact that Avoid this wordy substitute for *except that.*

expletive The dummy subjects *it* and *there* used to fill a grammatical slot in a sentence. ***It*** *is raining outside.* ***There*** *should be a law against it.*

explicit/implicit Both are adjectives; *explicit* means "stated outright," while *implicit* means just the opposite, "unstated."

farther/further *Farther* refers to physical distance; *further* refers to time or other abstract concepts.

fewer/less Use *fewer* with what can be counted and *less* with what cannot be counted.

flunk In formal writing, avoid this colloquial substitute for *fail.*

fragment A group of words beginning with a capital letter and ending with a period that looks like a sentence but lacks a subject or a predicate or both (see Section 22a).

further See **farther/further**.

gerund An *-ing* form of a verb used as a noun, such as *running, skiing,* or *laughing.*

good/well *Good* is an adjective and is not interchangeable with the adverb *well.* The one exception is health. Both she feels *good* and she feels *well* are correct.

hanged/hung Use *hanged* to refer only to executions; *hung* is used for all other instances.

have/of *Have*, not *of*, follows *should, could, would, may, must,* and *might.*

he/she; s/he Try to avoid language that appears to exclude either gender (unless this is intended, of course) and awkward compromises such as *he/she* or *s/he.* The best solution is to make pronouns plural (the gender-neutral *they*) wherever possible (see Section 25c).

helping verb See **auxiliary verb**.

hopefully This adverb is commonly used as a sentence modifier, but many readers object to it.

illusion See **allusion/illusion**.

immigrate See **emigrate from/immigrate to**.

imperative A sentence that expresses a command. Usually the subject is implied rather than stated.

implicit See **explicit/implicit**.

imply/infer *Imply* means to "suggest"; *infer* means to "draw a conclusion."

in regards to Avoid this wordy substitute for *regarding.*

incredible/incredulous *Incredible* means "unbelievable"; *incredulous* means "not believing."

independent clause See **main clause**.

indirect object A noun, pronoun, or noun clause that names who or what is affected by the action of a transitive verb.

infinitive The word *to* plus the base verb form: *to believe, to feel, to act.* See also **split infinitive**.

infinitive phrase A phrase that uses the infinitive form of a verb.

interjection A word expressing feeling that is grammatically unconnected to a sentence, such as *cool, wow, ouch,* or *yikes.*

interrogative A sentence that asks a question.

intransitive verb A verb that does not take an object, such as *sleep, appear,* or *laugh* (see Sections 24c and 28c).

irregardless Nonstandard for *regardless.*

irregular verb A verb that does not use either *-d* or *-ed* to form the past tense and past participle (see Section 24b).

it is my opinion that Avoid this wordy substitute for *I believe that.*

its/it's *Its* is the possessive of *it* and does not take an apostrophe; *it's* is the contraction for *it is.*

-ize/-wise The suffix *-ize* changes a noun or adjective into a verb (*harmony, harmonize*). The suffix *-wise* changes a noun or adjective into an adverb (*clock, clockwise*). Some writers are tempted to use these suffixes to convert almost any word into an adverb or verb form. Unless the word appears in a dictionary, don't use it.

kind of/sort of/type of Avoid using these colloquial expressions if you mean *somewhat* or *rather. It's kind of hot* is nonstandard. Each is permissible, however, when it refers to a classification of an object. Be sure that it agrees in number with the object it is modifying.

lay/lie *Lay* means "place" or "put" and generally takes a direct object (see Section 24c). Its main forms are *lay, laid, laid. Lie* means "recline" or "be positioned" and does not take an object. Its main forms are *lie, lay, lain.*

less See **fewer**.

lie See **lay/lie**.

linking verb A verb that connects the subject to the complement, such as *appear, be, feel, look, seem,* or *taste.*

lots/lots of Nonstandard in formal writing; use *many* or *much* instead.

main clause A group of words with a subject and a predicate that can stand alone as a sentence. Also called an *independent clause.*

mankind This term offends some readers and is outdated. Use *humans, humanity,* or *people* instead.

may/can See **can/may**.

may be/maybe *May be* is a verb phrase; *maybe* is an adverb.

media This is the plural form of the noun *medium* and requires a plural verb.

might of See **have/of**.

modal A kind of auxiliary verb that indicates ability, permission, intention, obligation, or probability, such as *can, could, may, might, must, shall, should, will,* or *would.*

modifier A general term for adjectives, adverbs, phrases, and clauses that describe other words (see Chapter 27).

must of See **have/of**.

noncount noun A noun that names things that cannot be counted, such as *air, energy,* or *water* (see Section 28a).

nonrestrictive modifier A modifier that is not essential to the meaning of the word, phrase, or clause it modifies and should be set off by commas or other punctuation (see Section 29c).

noun The name of a person, place, thing, concept, or action. See also **common noun** and **proper noun** (see Section 28a).

noun clause A subordinate clause that functions as a noun.

number See **amount/number**.

object Receiver of the action within the clause or phrase.

OK, O.K., okay Informal; avoid using in academic and professional writing. Each spelling is accepted in informal usage.

owing to the fact that Avoid this wordy, colloquial substitute for *because.*

parallelism The principle of putting similar elements or ideas in similar grammatical form (see Section 20c).

participle A form of a verb that uses *-ing* in the present (*laughing, playing*) and usually *-ed* or *-en* in the past (*laughed, played*). See Section 24a. Participles are either part of the verb phrase (*She had played the game before*) or used as adjectives (*the laughing girl*).

participial phrase A phrase formed either by a present participle (for example, *racing*) or by a past participle (for example, *taken*).

parts of speech The eight classes of words according to their grammatical function: nouns, pronouns, verbs, adjectives, adverbs, prepositions, conjunctions, and interjections.

passive A clause with a transitive verb in which the subject is being acted upon (see Section 18a). See also **active**.

people/persons *People* refers to a general group; *persons* refers to a collection of individuals. Use *people* over *persons* except when you're emphasizing the idea of separate persons within the group.

per Try not to use the English equivalent of this Latin word except in technical writing or familiar usages like *miles per gallon.*

phenomena This is the plural form of *phenomenon* ("observable fact" or "unusual event") and takes plural verbs.

phrase A group of words that does not contain both a subject and predicate.

plenty In academic and professional writing, avoid this colloquial substitute for *very*.

plus Do not use *plus* to join clauses or sentences. Use *and, also, moreover, furthermore*, or another conjunctive adverb instead.

precede/proceed Both are verbs but they have different meanings: *precede* means "come before," and *proceed* means "go ahead" or "continue."

predicate The part of the clause that expresses the action or tells something about the subject. The predicate includes the verb and all its complements, objects, and modifiers.

prejudice/prejudiced *Prejudice* is a noun; *prejudiced* is an adjective.

preposition A class of words that indicate relationships and qualities.

prepositional phrase A phrase formed by a preposition and its object, including the modifiers of its object.

pronoun A word that stands for other nouns or pronouns. Pronouns have several subclasses, including personal pronouns, possessive pronouns, demonstrative pronouns, indefinite pronouns, relative pronouns, interrogative pronouns, reflexive pronouns, and reciprocal pronouns (Chapter 25).

pronoun case Pronouns that function as the subjects of sentences are in the **subjective** case (*I, you, he, she, it, we, they*). Pronouns that function as direct or indirect objects are in the **objective** case (*me, you, him, her, it, us, them*). Pronouns that indicate ownership are in the **possessive** case (*my, your, his, her, its, our, their*) (see Section 25a).

proper noun A noun that names a particular person, place, thing, or group (see Section 28a). Proper nouns are capitalized.

question as to whether/question of whether Avoid these wordy substitutes for *whether*.

raise/rise The verb *raise* means "lift up" and takes a direct object. Its main forms are *raise, raised, raised.* The verb *rise* means "get up" and does not take a direct object. Its main forms are *rise, rose, risen.*

real/really Avoid using *real* as if it were an adverb. *Really* is an adverb; *real* is an adjective.

reason is because Omit either *reason is* or *because* when explaining causality.

reason why Avoid using this redundant combination.

relative pronoun A pronoun that initiates clauses, such as *that, which, what, who, whom,* or *whose.*

restrictive modifier A modifier that is essential to the meaning of the word, phrase, or clause it modifies (see Section 29c). Restrictive modifiers are usually not set off by punctuation.

rise/raise See **raise/rise**.

run-on sentence Two main clauses fused together without punctuation or a conjunction, appearing as one sentence (see Section 22b).

sentence A grammatically independent group of words that contains at least one main clause.

sentence fragment See **fragment**.

set/sit *Set* means "put" and takes a direct object; its main forms are *set, set, set. Sit* means "be seated" and does not take a direct object; its main forms are *sit, sat, sat. Sit* should not be used as a synonym for *set.*

shall/will *Shall* is used most often in first person questions, while *will* is a future tense helping verb for all persons. British English consistently uses *shall* with first person: *I shall, we shall.*

should of See **have/of**.

sit/set See **set/sit**.

some time/sometime/sometimes *Some time* means "a span of time," *sometime* means "at some unspecified time," and *sometimes* means "occasionally."

somebody/some body; someone/some one *Somebody* and *someone* are indefinite pronouns and have the same meaning. In *some body, body* is a noun modified by *some,* and in *some one, one* is a pronoun or adjective modified by *some.*

sort of See **kind of/sort of/type of**.

split infinitive An infinitive with a word or words between *to* and the base verb form, such as *to boldly go, to better appreciate.*

stationary/stationery *Stationary* means "motionless"; *stationery* means "writing paper."

subject A noun, pronoun, or noun phrase that identifies what the clause is about and connects with the predicate.

subject–verb agreement See **agreement**.

subordinate A relationship of unequal importance, in terms of either grammar or meaning (see Section 20a).

subordinate clause A clause that cannot stand alone but must be attached to a main clause. Also called a *dependent clause.*

subordinating conjunction A word that introduces a subordinate clause. Common subordinating conjunctions are *after, although, as, because, before, if, since, that, unless, until, when, where,* and *while.*

such Avoid using *such* as a synonym for *very. Such* should always be followed by *that* and a clause that contains a result.

sure A colloquial term used as an adverb to mean "certainly." Avoid using it this way in formal writing.

sure and/sure to; try and/try to *Sure to* and *try to* are correct; do not use *and* after *sure* or *try.*

take See **bring/take**.

that/which *That* introduces a restrictive or essential clause. Restrictive clauses describe an object that must be that particular object and no other. Though some writers occasionally use *which* with restrictive clauses, it is most often used to introduce nonrestrictive clauses. These are clauses that contain additional nonessential information about the object (see Section 29c).

transition A word or phrase that notes movement from one unit of writing to another.

transitive verb A verb that takes a direct object (see Section 24c).

verb A word that expresses action or characterizes the subject in some way. Verbs can show tense and mood (see Chapter 24 and Section 28c).

verbal A form of a verb used as an adjective, adverb, or noun. See also **gerund, infinitive, participle**.

well/good See **good/well**.

which/that See **that/which**.

who/whom *Who* and *whom* follow the same rules as other pronouns: *Who* is the subject pronoun; *whom* is the object pronoun (see Section 25a).

will/shall See **shall/will**.

-wise/-ize See **-ize/-wise**.

would of See **have/of**.

you Avoid indefinite uses of *you.* It should only be used to mean "you, the reader."

your/you're The two are not interchangeable. *Your* is the possessive form of "you"; *you're* is the contraction of "you are."

Index

A

D

E

Y

Z

Credits

Text Credits

"Kelty Traveling Fact" screen capture as appeared on Christopher Kelty website, www.kelty.org. Reprinted with permission of Christopher M. Kelty.

Sample journal cover and first page from "Reimagining the Functional Side of Computer Literacy" from *Journal of the Conference on College Composition and Communication*, Vol. 55, No. 3, February 2004.

Sample journal table of contents and article page from "Practicing Engineers Talk about the Importance of Talk: A Report on the Role of Oral Communication in the Workplace" by Ann L. Darling and Deanna P. Dannels, *Communication Education*, Vol. 52, Issue 1, January 2003, copyright © National Communication Association, reprinted by permission of (Taylor & Francis Ltd., http://www.tandf.co.uk/journals) on behalf of The National Communication Association.

Sample title page and detail of copyright page: Howard Gardner. *Five Minds for the Future*. Watertown: Harvard Business School Publishing, 2007.

Sample title page and detail of copyright page. From *How Cities Work: Suburbs, Sprawl, and the Roads Not Taken* by Alex Marshall, Copyright © 2000. Courtesy of the University of Texas Press.

Screen capture of article "Slave to the Boob Tube" from Salon.com website, www.salon.com.

Screen capture "Big Philanthropy" reprinted with permission from *The Wilson Quarterly*, Winter 2007. Copyright © 2007 by The Woodrow Wilson International Center for Scholars.

Screen capture from *The Wilson Quarterly*. Reprinted with permission from *The Wilson Quarterly*, Autumn 2007. Copyright © 2007 by The Woodrow Wilson International Center for Scholars.

Screen Capture "James Gandolfini" from Wikipedia, en.wikipedia.org. Copyright © 2007, Free Software Foundation, Inc., 51 Franklin Street, Fifth Floor, Boston, MA 02110-1301 USA. Everyone is permitted to copy and distribute verbatim copies of this license document, but changing it is not allowed.

Screen capture archive search from the LexisNexis website, www.lexisnexis.com. Copyright 2008 LexisNexis, a division of Reed Elsevier Inc. All Rights Reserved. LexisNexis and the Knowledge Burst logo are registered trademarks of Read Elsevier Properties Inc. and are used with the permission of LexisNexis.

Screen capture of LexisNexis archive search of *The Washington Post* article, from the LexisNexis website, www.lexisnexis.com. Copyright 2006 LexisNexis, a division of Reed Elsevier Inc. All Rights Reserved. LexisNexis and the Knowledge Burst logo are registered trademarks of Reed Elsevier Properties Inc. and are used with the permission of LexisNexis.

Screen capture of LexisNexis archive search of *The Washington Post* article, from the LexisNexis website, www.lexisnexis.com. Copyright 2008 LexisNexis, a division of Reed Elsevier Inc. All Rights Reserved. LexisNexis and the Knowledge Burst logo are registered trademarks of Reed Elsevier Properties Inc. and are used with the permission of LexisNexis.

Screen capture from *The Wilson Quarterly*. Reprinted with permission from *The Wilson Quarterly*, Winter 2007. Copyright © 2007 by The Woodrow Wilson International Center for Scholars.

Photo Credits

p. 7 Library of Congress

p. 60 Lowe Worldwide

p. 151 Frank Whigham

All other photos are from the author © Lester Faigley Photos.

REVISION GUIDE

Commonly used editing and proofreading symbols are listed here, along with references to the relevant chapters and sections of this handbook.

Words, Sentences, and Paragraphs

abbr	Abbreviation problem: 35c
adj	Adjective problem: 27a-b
adv	Adverb problem: 27a, 27c
agr	Agreement problem, either subject-verb or pronoun-antecedent: 23, 25b
apos	Apostrophe missing or misused: 32
art	Article is missing or misused: 28b
cap	Capitalization is needed: 35a
case	Case of a pronoun is incorrect: 25a
coh	Coherence lacking in a paragraph: 5a
cs	Comma splice occurs: 22c
dm	Dangling modifier appears: 27e
frag	Fragment instead of complete sentence: 22a
ital	Italics missing or misused: 35b
lc	Lower case needed: 35a
mm	Misplaced modifier: 27b-c
num	Number problem: 35e
p	Punctuation problem: 29-34
pass	Passive voice misused: 18a
pl	Plural form misused or needed: 28a
pron	Pronoun problem: 25
ref	Reference of a pronoun unclear: 25d
run-on	Run-on sentence problem: 22b
sexist	Sexist language: 21e
sp	Spelling needs to be checked: 6d
sub	Subordination is faulty: 20a
trans	Transition misused or needed: 6c
vb	Verb problem: 24
w	Wordy: 19
ww	Wrong word: 21
¶	Paragraph break needed: 5
no ¶	No paragraph break needed: 5
//	Parallelism needs to be checked: 20c

Punctuation and Mechanics

^,	Comma needed: 29
'	Apostrophe needed: 32
" "	Quotation marks needed: 33
⊙	Period needed: 34a
?	Question mark needed: 34b
!	Exclamation point needed: 34c
—	Dash needed: 31
. . .	Ellipses needed: 34e
( )	Parentheses needed: 31
[ ]	Brackets needed: 34d
#	Add a space
⁀	Close up a space
~	Delete this
^	Insert something
∽	Transpose (switch the order)

Contents

PART 1 Composing

PART 2 Researching

PART 3 Documentation